You Can Lead A Horse To Water But You Can't Make 'em Cha-Cha

Why Some People Stay In Abusive Relationships And Some Don't

KRISTINE GODINEZ, LPC

Bulk Orders
www.ahacounselingaz.com

Copyright ©2017 Kristine Godinez

First Edition, 2017

ISBN: 978-1977679055

"You gain strength, courage and confidence by every experience in which you really stop to look fear in the face.

You are able to say to yourself, 'I have lived through this horror. I can take the next thing that comes along.' You must do the thing you think you cannot do."

ELEANOR ROOSEVELT

TABLE OF CONTENTS

Acknowledgements 7

Foreword 9

1: What the Actual. . .? 15

2: Abusers Who Are Narcissists...26

3: The Abusers Who Are Borderlines 47

4: Anti-Social Personality Disordered Abusers 69

5: The Targets...83

6: Codependent/People Pleaser Targets............................86

7: Trauma Bonding and Stockholm Syndrome Targets........98

8: Toxic Parents and Grandparents...................................117

9: Religious Abuse 130

10: Totally Addicted to Attachment Styles? 151

11: Abuse by Proxy and Parental Alienation....................167

12: Abuse in the Workplace 185

13: A Tale of Two Empath Targets 201

14: What It Boils Down To...222

ACKNOWLEDGMENTS

To my husband, John, who is my rock. To Laura Witte and Lauren Archibeque and Diane Brown, who are never afraid to tell me what I need to hear. To Stephen Gresser, you made a huge difference in my life and taught me more than you realize. To Lynne McAllen, my sister from another mister. To Terry Burgoyne, my sister and my voice of reason. To Andy Brenits and Bryan Hartzell, thank you for pushing me to get this book done in a ridiculously short amount of time. To Shahein Nadjafi, my photographer: Damn, baby! You made me look good!!!

FOREWORD

If you read my first book, *What's Wrong With Your Dad?* you will know that I write how I talk, swear words and humor and all. I believe in making things accessible to everyone. I believe in being real and authentic and unapologetically me. I will use case studies in this book, but I promise you it will not be a psychobabble of terms and citations, although I will include the websites and books that I pulled my information from so you can read up on abuse for yourselves. The situations I write about are universal and will resonate with anyone who has been abused or knows someone who has been abused mainly because no matter where in the world the abuser is, the abuse and the patterns of abuse are the same.

All case studies are conglomerations of cases; all names and identifying characteristics have been changed. So again, if you are easily offended by swear words or feel that someone cannot be professional and have a sense of humor or swear, or both, do us both a favor and put this book down now. If, however, you are ready for some come-to-Jesus-real-shit on abuse, personality disorders, and abuse syndrome, keep reading.

We are all hearing psychology buzzwords these days: "President So and So is such a narcissist!" "God! The news makes me so sad because I'm such an empath!" "Jeezus, she is SO borderline!" But, really, what is a true narcissist? What is a true empath? What really is a borderline? Why do empaths and personality disordered people seem to find each other in what turns out to be a massively toxic relationship? Can you actually help someone leave abuse or is the target doomed to repeat the abuse over and over and over again? How do the different types of narcissism play out with an empath? How do different types of borderline behaviors play out with an empath? I will be using case studies to illustrate what is going on. Also, the stereotype is that men are narcissists and women are borderline but absolutely nothing could be further from the truth. Both men and women can have either or both behavior types, and women can absolutely be the abuser.

I have desperate family members and friends of the targets begging me to tell them that their loved one will come around and be alright. They want me to tell them that they will awaken from the F.O.G. (Fear, Obligation, Guilt) and return to sanity. I wish I could tell them that they all will, but I cannot. Some will be able to dance the Cha Cha of returning to sanity. Some will not.

I should probably get a bunch of definitions out of the way so you understand what the heck I'm talking about. When you read about abuse, you are going to be confronted with a bunch of terms and acronyms:

Abuse amnesia: When either the abuser denies having abused someone, either physically or emotionally, or conversely, the target of abuse "forgets" about having been abused or "forgets" information that informs them that they are being abused *(http://outofthefog.website/what-not-to-do-1/2015/12/3/abuse-amnesia)*

Abuse by proxy: When the abuser uses either the target of abuse or other flying monkeys to abuse the friends and family who are the targets greatest support in an effort to isolate the target— and the target doesn't even realize that they are doing it! *(http://flyingmonkeysdenied .com/2016/02/09/dark-triads-use-abuse-by-proxy-tactic-to-enact-revenge-on-victims/)*

ASPD: Anti-Social Personality Disorder (DSM-5)

BPD: Borderline Personality Disorder (DSM-5)

Cluster B: Personality disorders are broken into three distinct groups: Cluster A (Paranoid, Schizoid, Schizotypal), Cluster B (Anti-Social, Borderline, Histrionic, Narcissistic), and Cluster C (Avoidant, Dependent, Obsessive Compulsive); you will find the majority of abusers in the Cluster B group (DSM-5)

Codependent: Unhealthy clinging and needing another person *(http://www.webmd.com/sex-relationships/features/signs-of-a-codependent-relationship#1)*

Dark triad: A person with malignant narcissistic personality disorder, psychopathy, and Machiavellianism; in other words, no empathy or conscience *(https://www.psychologytoday .com/ blog/fulfillment-any-age/201301/shedding-light-psychology-s-dark-triad;* see also *https://www.psychologytoday.com/blog/ fulfillment-any-age/201706/why-psychopaths-dont-care-if-they-hurt-you)*

DSM-5: Diagnostic and Statistical Manual of Mental Disorders, Fifth Edition (basically, the Bible for mental health professionals)

Empath: One who feels and takes on others emotions *(https:// www.psychologytoday.com /blog/emotional-freedom/201602/10-traits-empathic-people-share)*

Flying monkeys: People who carry out the abuser's abuse and/or enable the abuser to continue abusing *(https://pro.psychcentral. com/recovery-expert/2016/07/the-narcissists-flying-monkeys/)*

Gaslighting: Based on the play and the movie Gaslight with Ingrid Bergman, it is a lay term for pathological lying and rewriting of history with the intent to manipulate and control *(https:// www.psychologytoday.com/blog/here-there-and-everywhere/201701/11-signs-gaslighting-in-relationship)*

Intermittent Positive Re enforcement: How abusers control through being kind, then cruel, then cruel, then kind, to keep the target of abuse trying to please them and off balance *(http:// psychopathsandlove.com/intermittent-reinforcement/)*

Love bombing: "Love bombing is an attempt to influence another person with over-the-top displays of attention and affection. We're not just talking about romantic gestures, like flowers and trips. Love bombing invariably includes lots of romantic conversation, long talks about 'our future,' and long periods of staring into each other's eyes. It's the combination of words and deeds that makes love bombing so powerful, especially considering today's technology. The ability to call, text, email, or connect on social media 24/7 makes it easier to be in constant contact with the object of one's affection than ever before." *(https://www.psychologytoday.com/blog/reading-between-the-headlines/201703/love-bombing-have-you-ever-been-the-target)*

Machiavellian: Control freak based on the writer of The Prince, which was a despot's handbook in 1513 AD *(https://en.wikipedia. org/wiki/The_Prince)*

Malignant: Two definitions and both apply: 1. Spiteful, malicious, malevolent, evil-intentioned, vindictive, vengeful, nasty, hurtful, wounding, cruel, unkind and 2. Virulent, infectious, invasive, uncontrollable, dangerous, deadly, incurable *(https://www. merriam-webster.com/dictionary /malignant)*

Mind control/brainwashing: Influencing the target of abuse using manipulation and gaslighting to convince the target to do what the abuser wants both physically and emotionally *(http:// www. decision-making-confidence.com/mind-control.html)*

Narcissistic Abuse Syndrome: The pattern of behavior in which a target gets hooked by and remains or returns to abuse; it really should be called Abused Brain Syndrome because people abused by ANY abuser narcissistic or not show the same pattern of behavior *(https://blogs .psychcentral.com/relationships/2017/03/ narcissistic-abuse-and-the-symptoms-of-narcissist-victim-syndrome/; see also http://narcissisticbehavior.net/narcissistic-victim-syndrome-what-the-heck-is-that/)*

NPD: Narcissistic Personality Disorder (DSM-5)

Picking up fleas from the abuser: The target begins "mirroring" or behaving EXACTLY like the abuser in a misguided attempt to please the abuser and stay off the radar *(https:// joyfulalivewoman.com/2010/01/17/fleas-bad-behavior-patterns-*

and-habits-picked-up-from-living-with-a-narcissist/)

Psychopathy: A more malignant form of Anti-Social Personality Disorder

Stockholm syndrome: Named for the bank heist in 1973 in which the hostages formed a trauma bond with their hostage takers *(http://counsellingresource.com/therapy/self-help/stockholm/)*

Target: The person the abuser has in their sights to abuse

Trauma bond: Intermittent positive rewards coupled with emotional abuse, which causes the target to rely on the abuser *(https://pro.psychcentral.com/recovery-expert/2015/10/what-is-trauma-bonding/)*

Word salad: When the abuser is caught in abuse or maladaptive behavior so the person twists what happened, turns the subject back to how the target is at fault, and do circular arguments *(https://www.psychopathfree.com/articles/10-warning-signs-of-word-salad.147/)*

Excellent! Now that you have some definitions, let's move on to the main topic.

"I am living in hell from one day to the next.
But there is nothing I can do to escape.
I don't know where I would go if I did.
I feel utterly powerless, and that feeling is my prison.
I entered of my own free will, I locked the door,
and I threw away the key."

Haruki Murakami

❶

WHAT THE ACTUAL...?

One of the most frustrating things to live through is seeing someone you love return to abuse and gallop off at full speed toward a cliff, all the while flipping family and friends off and telling you, the family, and/or friends that you are full of shit and are the problem. Sigh. This book could have been named so many different things. "Sometimes you're the bug, sometimes you're the windshield" or "WHAT THE FUCK ARE YOU DOING????!!!" Yeah. So many different titles that encompass watching someone you love either return to their abuser or pick out a new abuser.

The other title would be "The Dance of Death Between the Personality Disordered and the Empath." Too dramatic? No. Not really, not when you consider the statistics for domestic violence. According to the National Domestic Violence Hotline, "3 in 10 women and 1 in 10 men experience stalking, physical or emotional abuse by a partner that resulted in an impact on their functioning." Study after study discusses the negative emotional and physical effects abuse has on the target's mental and physical functioning. *(https://www.domesticshelters.org / domestic-violence-articles-information/men-can-be-abused-too#.WWOHy9PyvFR)*

In extreme cases of abuse, the victim is killed by their abuser either directly or, more sinisterly, indirectly. "How?" you ask. The abuser encourages unhealthy behavior and lifestyle choices such as not exercising, smoking, demanding that the person eat unhealthy food such as an abuser encouraging a person with diabetes to eat sweets, or encouraging the target to use illegal drugs and overindulge in alcohol. Show me a malignant abuser, and I will show you someone who claims to love the target but, in truth, is trying to kill them by inches. *(https:// www. psychologytoday.com/blog/the-human-equation/201708/if-i-cant-have-you-no-one-can)*

"WHY?" you ask. "WHY would someone return to or pick out a new abuser and place themselves, their health, their happiness, and their life at risk? Why would they turn their back on family and friends who clearly love them and want them to be healthy? Why would they refuse to go see a counselor?" Short answer: Abuse syndrome. Long answer: Codependency, addiction, cognitive dissonance, ego, pride, low self-esteem or no self-esteem, Stockholm syndrome, backlash effect, and the unconscious messages received from caregivers in childhood.

Although abuse syndrome is not yet included in the Diagnostic and Statistical Manual of Mental Disorders, Fifth Edition (DSM-5), there are similarities in the cluster of behaviors across all cultures that cannot be ignored in the targets of abuse. Some clinicians argue that it should be called narcissistic abuse syndrome. However, targets of malignant borderlines and anti-social or psychopathic abuse also have the exact same cluster of maladaptive behaviors. *(https:// blogs.psychcentral.com/ relationships/2017/03/narcissistic-abuse-and-the-symptoms-of-narcissist-victim-syndrome/)*

Abusers—whether they have Narcissistic Personality Disorder (NPD), Borderline Personality Disorder (BPD), or Anti-Social Personality Disorder (ASPD)—all use the same language and the same manipulations to gain control over their target and take their will away from them. Those manipulations include gaslighting, lying, rewriting history, guilt tripping, intimidation, raging, veiled threats, using word salad, constant criticism or dissatisfaction no matter what the target does to please them, and isolating the target from friends and family. The abuser's goal is to keep the target of abuse in an emotional F.O.G. (commonly known as Fear. Obligation. Guilt.) so that the targets are unable to escape the abuser. *(https://www.psychologytoday.com/blog / evolution-the-self/201404/the-vampire-s-bite-victims-narcissists-speak-out)*

Most people, outside of clinicians, are flummoxed as to how an empathic, intelligent, kind, and loving person could fall for and stay in an abusive relationship, much less how they could return to or seek out another abusive relationship. It is hard for family and friends to wrap their heads around how abusers behave and how the target of abuse becomes what can best be described as an abuser's zombie. The target of abuse looks like the family member or friend you know and love, but they are slowly being changed by the abuser to fit the abuser's image of themselves. Why? Because abusers are inherently fearful, morbidly insecure, jealous, and weak; they must have everyone parrot back to them their own mistaken thoughts and beliefs. Otherwise, their fragile sense of self is threatened. *(https://www.psychologytoday.com / articles/199803/anatomy-violent-relationship)*

Dissention is not seen as a healthy discourse in their relationships; it is seen as a betrayal. Abusers will then emotionally and sometimes physically punish the person with differing opinions or thoughts. *(https://www.psychologytoday. com/blog/hurt-people-hurt-people/201510/five-reasons-people-abuse-their-partners)* The target of abuse learns quickly to conform so they do not get punished, losing little bits and pieces of themselves along the way as they shove who they are further and further away and take on the personality traits of the abuser. This is known as picking up fleas from the abuser in common terms, and as identification with the aggressor as far as a defense mechanism goes. What happens is that the target is either consciously or subconsciously afraid of the abuser and will eventually begin adopting the behavior and spouting the rhetoric of the abuser to the point in which the target of abuse is no longer recognizable to family and friends. *(https://www. psychologytoday.com/blog/the-almost-effect/201510/donald-*

trump-and-identification-the-aggressor; see also Ferenczi, S. [1933], The Confusion of Tongues Between Adults and Children: The Language of Tenderness and Passion. International Journal of Psychoanalysis, 30: 4, 1949 [English translation version])

Confused? Let me give you a case study to illustrate what is going on. All identifying traits and names have been changed.

Jenny, age 30, a stay-at-home mom with two kids, a boy, age 8, and a girl, age 10. Was committed to a mental hospital due to a suicide attempt. Was seeing me for the required follow-up.

Me: "Hey Jenny! How are you doing?"

Jenny: (Looking confused) "Me? I'm fine."

Me: (Cocking my head and smiling) "Is that a counselor's fine or are you really ok?"

Jenny: "What is a counselor's fine?"

Me: (smiling) "Well, when someone says they are "fine" to a counselor, it usually stands for fucked up, insecure, neurotic, and emotional."

Jenny: (Laughing) "Yes. I meant a counselor's fine."

Me: "So, I hear you tried to do an early checkout from the planet."

Jenny: (Looking ashamed) "Yes."

Me: (Getting her to look up) "Hey, listen. All it means is that you are in a great deal of emotional pain. That's it. No guilt. No judgment. No shame."

Jenny: (Distressed) "I have two babies. I don't know what I was thinking! They would be left with him."

Me: "Tell me more."

Jenny: "Jess and I got married right out of high school. He was always so jealous. I don't have any friends. He chased them all away. Either they were too slutty or he didn't like their spouses or he just didn't want me to go out with them because when I did he would accuse me of 'slutting' around. But he continued to go hang out with his coworkers and friends."

Me: "Sounds very lonely. "

Jenny: "He was even jealous of my old boss. So when I got pregnant with Jessica, our oldest, he told me I could stay at home, not work, and raise the baby. That sounded good, at first. As soon as Jessica was born, he stopped helping. He never changed a diaper or stayed up with her when she was colicky. He stopped helping around the house. He put me on an allowance and told me since I wasn't "contributing," I couldn't spend any money. The money he gave me was barely enough to buy groceries and gas. He transferred all our money into his account, and I have no access to anything."

Me: (Frowning) "What you are describing to me sounds like financial abuse."

Jenny: (Her eyes lighting up for the first time, recognizing that I saw what she was going through) "It was! It is! I got pregnant with our youngest, Mitch, and it got worse. It was like I was a single mom except I had three kids. He would get jealous if I showed the kids love when he was around. One time he even said that I paid more attention to our cat than I did to him, which is ridiculous."

Me: "So he is jealous of anyone, even his own children and pet, if you show anyone other than him affection?"

Jenny: "Yes! One day after he raged about Zoey, our cat, she suddenly disappeared, and he didn't seem to care! When I got pregnant with Mitch, he would get angry any time I had to go to the doctor for a checkup. Then after Mitch was born, he wouldn't raise the allowance I was given even though we had a new baby. He would fly into rages and tell me that I agreed to be on an allowance and that I told him he didn't have to help when I asked him for help. (Looking at me desperately) I never agreed to any of that except to stay home and be an at-home mom."

Me: (Now feeling very concerned, given the cat disappeared) "I believe you. Sounds like he rewrote history and was gaslighting you. Do you think he had anything to do with Zoey's disappearance?"

Jenny: "Yes. I do. I think he either drove her out somewhere and dumped her or killed her. He insinuated he did something to her but wouldn't say what. He changes his stories all the time! He tells me I said things that I didn't say or that I didn't say things that I did say. He describes entire events that I know never happened until I sit there and question my sanity! He constantly tells me I am crazy!"

Me: "What you are describing is gaslighting. It is a term named for a play and a movie in which the villain tries to drive the woman in the movie insane by lying to her about the lights in the house being dimmed or on full so that she thinks she is losing her mind."

Jenny: "That's me! I caught him having affairs, and he would twist it around and start blaming me for the affair by saying the kids were driving him crazy or the house was a mess so it was all my fault!"

Me: (Nodding) "Common tactic for an abuser."

Jenny: "You think I was abused?"

Me: "What do you think?"

Jenny: "He would scream at me for hours. Keep me up at night. Accuse me of sleeping with neighbors, people at the grocery store, my OB/GYN. I couldn't go anywhere. But then when he was done screaming, he said he was jealous because he loved me so much and because I'm so beautiful. He tried to keep my family from being able to contact me. If I went out with them, he would demand to go along, too, because he didn't want them to be 'bad-mouthing and putting ideas in my head.'"

Me: "What does your family think of him?"

Jenny: "My sister said he was an abuser. So did my mom and my aunt."

Me: (Gently prodding) "You avoided my original question. What do you think?"

Jenny: (Scrunching her face up and then when she spoke it was like a dam bursting) "This isn't normal! I don't like the way I feel! He is abusing me!" (She gasped and then followed almost immediately as if she were afraid of her abuser being in the room) "But he is a great dad, and he provides really well. He is always sorry when he screams at me, and he tells me he loves me. I need to stay in the relationship! I can't do this alone! We've been together for years!"

Me: "Why did you try to take your life?" (recognizing the Stockholm syndrome and the time investment fallacy thinking; *https://www.psychologytoday.com/blog/dating-decisions/201402 /relationship-investments-double-edged-sword*)

Jenny: (Looking confused) "Because, because (Now bursting into tears) I don't know who I am anymore! I used to be happy, I loved who I was in high school. And now I look in the mirror and I hate myself."

Me: "Jenny, does he put you down? Is he verbally abusive? Does he hit you or throw things?"

Jenny: "He tells me all the time that I'm stupid and that I am a horrible housekeeper and mother. He tells me I'm crazy. He screams at me and shoves me if he doesn't get his way. Last week he picked up dishes off the counter and threw them at me. He missed, but it scared me."

Me: "Wow."

Jenny: "He is abusive, isn't he?"

Me: "Hon, if it hurts, it ain't love. What do you think?"

Jenny: "Why do you keep asking me?"

Me: "Because I know you already know the answer."

Jenny: (Gathering courage) "He has abused me since our last six months in high school."

Jenny had reached her rock bottom when Jess, her abusive spouse, had paraded his latest affair in front of her and the children and had brought the woman over to the house to meet the kids. Yeah. You read that right. He told her how he was going to take the kids from her and how she was worthless and crazy and that no judge would ever believe her if she tried to divorce him. He had undermined her self-esteem so much so that she believed him and, in a fit of despair, attempted suicide. Fortunately, her oldest found her mother in the bathtub and called police. Jenny had a long road to go in leaving Jess and had a couple more hospitalizations before she was stable enough to leave him and face the legal and emotional battle.

Jess's behavior was typical for a malignant narcissist in his scorched earth approach to the divorce. He wanted full custody and did not want to pay any child support, not because he was concerned for the well-being of the children or that he thought Jenny was a danger to them, but because he didn't want to give Jenny anything, even if it was for the children. As the divorce dragged on, mainly because Jess refused to be reasonable about anything and was representing himself in the divorce, Jess's true colors began to show through as he gave up more and more of his parenting time with the kids in order to go socialize. Jenny's attorney encouraged her to document all time given up by Jess. After keeping track, she had the kids way more than 50% of the time. When it became apparent to Jess that the judge was not going to go for full custody for him and that he would have only 50/50 custody and would also have to pay spousal support since he didn't allow Jenny to work for the last 13 years, out of spite, Jess quit his official job and began working under the table so it appeared that he had no money. Jenny's family stepped up to the plate and financially and emotionally supported her until she could get on her feet. Jenny hated sending the kids over to her ex's house for fear of how he would treat them. *(https://www. psychologytoday.com/blog/nurturing-resilience/201004/how-have-good-divorce-and-keep-your-kids-resilient)*

The kids would come home from a visit wearing old clothes that were too small. Jess would steal the new clothes she had bought for the kids and never send the new clothes back, forcing her to buy more new clothes each time. He also bad-mouthed Jenny to the kids every single time and tried to use the kids as flying monkeys to spy on Jenny and report back to him what she was doing and who she was seeing. *(https://www.psychologytoday. com/blog/the-new-grief/201110/helping-children-survive-divorce-three-critical-factors)* Jess continued to harass her until the kids were old enough to tell the court they wanted NOTHING to do with their father.

Jenny went back to school and became a social worker. She divorced him 10 years ago and was dragged back into court every year for 10 years—which, I am sad to say, is NOT an uncommon experience for people divorcing malignant abusers. Abusers need power and control. They would rather have an angry dysfunctional connection to someone than no connection at all. Eventually, she had to file an order of protection against him as did the now grown children.

Jenny was one of the lucky ones whose family and friends recognized that she was being isolated and abused, and they rallied to her when she needed them. Most family members and friends do not recognize abuse, especially if it is covert, and use the excuse for not intervening as "Well, they are both adults, they know what they are doing." WRONG! The abuser knows exactly what they are doing to manipulate and control, but the target of abuse has regressed and is in a F.O.G. (Fear, Obligation, and Guilt) fostered by their abuser. They are literally held hostage by their abuser through intermittent positive re enforcements, which means the abuser will be kind, then cruel, then cruel for a while, then kind for a while, and the abuser will do so INTENTIONALLY to keep the target on their toes, unbalanced emotionally and trying to please them and stay in their good graces. When the abuser is kind, the abuse victim feels on top of the world like they just climbed Mount Everest. When the abuser is cruel and harsh, the target is in an emotional hell and will work as hard as they can to get the abuser to "love" them again. The target of abuse is not operating on an "adult" level as you would recognize it. They are operating on the same emotional level as a child seeking the approval and love of a parent. Why? Because they are mirroring the abuser's emotional intelligence level, which tends to be that of a six-year-old at best. *(http://www.halcyon.com/jmashmun/npd/six.html)*

Frightened of what the abused go through? You should be. In the next couple of chapters let's look at who the abusers are and how they torture and manipulate their targets.

"Narcissism falls along the axis of what psychologists call personality disorders, one of a group that includes antisocial, dependent, histrionic, avoidant and borderline personalities. But by most measures, narcissism is one of the worst, if only because the narcissists themselves are so clueless."

Jeffrey Kluger

❷

ABUSERS WHO ARE NARCISSISTS

Most abusers have, well, putting it nicely, issues. Most have two or more issues going on with them. There is either addiction—whether that be to alcohol, drugs, sex, food, gambling, or some other addiction—and/or a coexisting or comorbid mental health condition such as a personality disorder, bi polar, or other mental health condition. *(https://www.psychologytoday .com/ articles/199803/anatomy-violent-relationship; see also https:// www.healthyplace.com /abuse/emotional-psychological-abuse/ emotionally-abusive-men-and-women-who-are-they)*

First, we must get some definitions out of the way. Is there a difference between a narcissist and someone with Narcissistic Personality Disorder? Yes. Someone can be full of themselves and arrogant but not personality disordered. They can be self-centered but still not personality disordered. *(https://www. psychologytoday.com/articles/200601/field-guide-narcissism)*

The clinical definition of Narcissistic Personality Disorder, taken straight out of the DSM-5, is this: having "a pervasive pattern of grandiosity (in fantasy or behavior), need for admiration and lack of empathy, beginning by early adulthood and present in a variety of contexts, as indicated by five (or more) of the following:

1. Has a grandiose sense of self-importance (e.g., exaggerates achievements and talents, expects to be recognized as superior without commensurate achievements).

2. Is preoccupied with fantasies of unlimited success, power,

brilliance, beauty, or ideal love.

3. Believes that he or she is "special" and unique and can only be understood by, or should associate with, other special or high-status people (or institutions).

4. Requires excessive admiration.

5. Has a sense of entitlement (i.e., unreasonable expectations of especially favorable treatment or automatic compliance with his or her expectations).

6. Is interpersonally exploitative (i.e., takes advantage of others to achieve his or her on ends).

7. Lacks empathy; is unwilling to recognize or identify with the feelings and needs of others.

8. Is often envious of others or believes that others are envious of him or her.

9. Shows arrogant, haughty behaviors or attitudes.

"Yes!" you say to yourself. "But what exactly is a narcissist? Are there different types of narcissistic personality disordered people?" Yes and no. It depends how far down the ego rabbit hole they have gone. It depends on what manipulation will work to get their wants and needs met. They can and they do flow between all three "types."

- Grandiose *(https://www.psychologytoday.com/ articles/201107/how-spot-narcissist)*

- Covert *(https://www.psychologytoday.com/blog/ communication-success/201601/7-signs-covert-introvert-narcissist)*

- Somatic *(http://flyingmonkeysdenied.com/2016/02/24/ somatic-narcissists-are-obsessed-with-appearance-and-status/)*

In layman's terms, a Grandiose narcissist has overt behavior. Grandiose narcissists scream to the world how awesome they are and demand that everyone agrees with their world view. Covert narcissists come across as fragile or shy or vulnerable; they are just as pathological but more introverted and therefore more likely to fly under the radar for a longer period of time. They are insidious—and in many ways more dangerous and damaging than the Grandiose narcissist. Somatic narcissists are concerned with appearance and the body; the way they abuse themselves and others is similar but different. However, remember that everything is on a spectrum from mere "traits of" sliding to Covert, sliding to Grandiose and eventually all the way to full blown malignant dark triad in which they actively hurt other people and enjoy it. If the person with the personality disorder(s) does not seek help, they will eventually slide into malignancy. *(https://www.psychologytoday.com/blog/neurosagacity/201702/malignant-narcissism-collision-two-personality-disorders)*

Let's start diving into the case studies to illustrate. All names and identifying details have been changed. We will start with the Grandiose type.

Peter, age 22, male. Dropped out of college. No romantic partner. No job. Lives with his parents. Very intelligent. Healthy weight.

Me: "Hi, Peter, what is going on in your life? How can I help you?"

Peter: "I need to be famous. Like right now!"

Me: "Um, ok. So what do you want to be famous for?"

Peter: "I don't know! I just need to be famous because I'm me! I'm brilliant! I am so smart. I never had to study anything during high school!"

Me: "Are you in college right now?"

Peter: (With an air of contempt) "Pfffft! College! I know more than any professor could possibly teach me! I don't need college! I dropped out!"

Me: "Are you working right now?"

Peter: (Again with an air of contempt) "I don't need a job! I deserve money for just being who I am! My parents pay for me! I am going to be famous for my rap music!"

Me: "You are 22 years old, you don't go to college, you have no career path, and your parents pay for all your living needs?"

Peter: (With a total air of entitlement) "Yeah. And they should."

Me: "Tell me about your parents."

Peter: (Shrugs) "Dad works in a cubicle and drives for Uber on the weekends. Mom works two part-time jobs."

Me: "And you are okay with that?"

Peter: (Rolling his eyes) "Yeah."

Me: "Ok, so tell me about your rap music."

Peter: "I do the best rap music in the world! Dr. Dre would hire me in a heartbeat!"

Me: "So have you written a rap song yet?"

Peter: "No. I hang out with all of these rappers in Scottsdale. They all say how talented I am!"

Me: (Recognizing magical thinking) "Okay. So the reality is that in order to make money and be famous, you have to actually write and perform."

Peter: (Ignoring what I just said) "They are all so jealous of me. You don't understand. I am better than they are."

Me: "So let me understand: You don't have a job, you don't have your own place, you haven't written any music, you hang out with rappers who are jealous of you, you haven't done anything to be famous, but you deserve to be famous?"

Peter: (Again rolling his eyes) "Duh! That's why I'm here! I want you to tell me how to be famous!"

Me: (Taken aback but not showing it) "Do you think it's fair that your parents work multiple jobs to support you as an adult?"

Peter: (Now glaring at me) "They want to cut me off and throw me out. (Returning to a smug look) They won't though. They feel too guilty."

And so it went for the rest of the session. He basically wanted me to tell him the quick and easy way to be famous. There was no way to reach this kid. He was so deep down the rabbit hole of magical thinking and ego defenses *(https://www. psychologytoday.com/blog/sideways-view/201510/ego-defence- mechanisms-the-work-anna-freud)*, truly believing that he should be adored for just being him, and he had no empathy for the fact that his parents were killing themselves working multiple jobs to keep him afloat—and he just didn't care.

At the end of the session, after having him ask multiple times how to be famous, I suggested to the client that he either return to school to work on a degree and/or get a job and take some ownership and responsibility for his life, and that he would actually have to start writing and performing and work for the "overnight" success and fame. The client stormed out, declaring he knew more about psychology than I did and he needed a more famous counselor.

That is an example of a Grandiose narcissist.

"Wait! What?" you say. "Adult kids can be narcissistically abusive to their parents?" Yessireebob! They sure as heck can! *(https://www.psychologytoday.com/conditions/elder-or-dependent-adult-abuse)* Nursing homes are filled with parents who have been and are being abused by narcissistic adult kids who are abusing them financially and verbally. If parents do not stop enabling an adult narcissist, being broke and alone in a nursing home is exactly what will end up happening to them.

Grandiose narcissists are often found in areas such as law enforcement, as judges, in politics, in the theater, and other professions in which people are in the public eye. On the flip side, you can also have a mundane job, such as a plumber, and be a Grandiose narcissist. It is all in the entitlement, the lack of empathy, and the repeated behavior. *(https://www. psychologytoday .com/articles/201107/how-spot-narcissist)*

Let me give one more example of a Grandiose narcissist. Again, all names and identifying characteristics have been changed.

Bertha, age 56, overweight, and balding, has the appearance of having eaten something sour, and Grant, age 55, also overweight, with dark circles under his eyes, looks like he has not slept in decades. Married 30 years. They are coming in for couples counseling.

Me: "Hey guys! How can I help you today?"

Bertha: "He can't do anything right!"

Grant: "Bertha!"

Bertha: (Now running with it since she has the floor) "He absolutely cannot do anything right! He keeps going off golfing! He should stay home with me!"

Grant: "And do what? Watch TV?"

Bertha: "Yes! Absolutely! You should be home with me watching TV! It is your job to keep me company!"

Grant: "Bertha I hate the shows you watch. Golfing keeps me fit, and I like to socialize."

Bertha: (Looking hurt) "You don't need anyone else but me!"

Me: "So, hi. (Waving at them) Sounds like expectations are not being met in this relationship."

Grant: "You can say that again! I do all of the housework, I make all of the money, and when I want to spend time golfing or spend my money on myself, Bertha comes unglued and starts crying that I don't love her." (The next was said almost pleading to me) "I DO love her!"

Bertha: "I gave you two beautiful children! I shouldn't have to do housework!"

Me: (In my head) "Wow. Sense of entitlement much?" (Outside my head) "So the relationship feels unbalanced to both of you?"

Grant and Bertha: "Yes!" (This would be the first and last time they agreed on anything in the session.)

Grant: "She couldn't be bothered to raise our children. She insisted on having a nanny."

Bertha: "And why shouldn't I have had a nanny? All of our friends had nannies helping them!"

Grant: "No, they didn't. She also insisted on having a maid service and a personal chef."

Bertha: "I deserve to be taken care of! You don't take care of me!"

Me: (Watching her swing from entitled to victim) "Okay. So, your kids are grown?"

Grant: "Yes, they've been out of the house for 10 years now."

Bertha: "They don't ever call or want to visit!"

Grant: "Well, you don't call or visit them either, it is a two way street."

Bertha: "I shouldn't have to call them! I'm their mother! They are ungrateful for all I've done for them!"

Grant: "You mean all their nanny did for them."

This went on, tit for tat the rest of the session. Bertha felt a sense of entitlement to Grant's money and time and her own children's time, so much so that when Grant tried to spend time and money on himself, she became enraged and accused him of not loving her. Or when the kids were busy, she accused them of being ingrates and tried to guilt trip them with how much she had sacrificed for them when, in fact, she had made no such sacrifice. But to her, giving up any of her time, her wants, her needs, was a sacrifice. In fact, in one session she actually yelled "What about my wants! My needs!" even though it was clear that Grant was the one giving up all of his wants and his needs due to his codependent tendencies. Bertha was grandiose in her entitlement and clear statements that she deserved to be treated with special favor, even though she had not done anything to merit special favor. Grant lamented how she treated the wait staff at restaurants during one session, and Bertha made it clear that the wait staff to her were somehow not human. All things that Grandiose narcissists do. Grant was not interested in leaving the relationship, only managing how to be able to stay married and still go golfing. He had long since resigned himself that he was going to die staying married to this woman. Self- esteem issues on his part? Probably. Codependent? Definitely.

Next, let's take a look at the Covert narcissist. Coverts share a lot of similarities with Grandiose narcissists except their personal storyline is that of the constant victim. They use a lot of word salad—that is, statements that sound like they are answering the question but not really. Let's take a look at another case study. Again, all names and identifying characteristics have been changed.

Caroline is a morbidly obese 36-year-old. She is a single mom with two teenage girls. She is a smoker. She has been divorced for over 12 years.

Me: "Hi, Caroline. What did you want to work on today?"

Caroline: (Sighing) "My ex is such a loser. He can barely make child support payments."

Me: "Is he late on his payments?"

Caroline: "No. He makes them, it's just, he works at a Circle K. He could make so much more but he won't."

Me: "So you feel he is working at a Circle K on purpose?"

Caroline: "He is doing it to spite me! If he made more money, I would get more money."

Me: "Well, Caroline, there isn't much we can do here in a session to change his job situation. What we can work on is the thought that is driving you crazy, which is that you believe him to be doing it on purpose."

Caroline: "He IS doing it on purpose! Being a single mom is hard! You don't understand! No one does! I don't have enough money to go out and date! I don't have enough money to do fun things! You want to do fun things! Everyone wants to do fun things! People do all sorts of fun things!"

Me: (Recognizing she is starting to use word salad) "What about for the girls?"

Caroline: (Dismissively) "The girls get to do all sorts of fun things but I don't!"

Me: "How many packs a day do you smoke?"

Caroline: "What has that got to do with anything? You get to go spend money on you! I should get to spend money on me! It's not fair, and life should be fair! You need life to be fair, don't you?"

Me: (Trying hard to stay on track with her) "I'm trying to find you extra money."

Caroline: "I'm not giving up my cigarettes! Or my Starbucks! Or eating out! People like to eat out! You like to eat out! I have a right to eat out if I want to!"

Me: "But you said you don't have enough money."

Caroline: (Switching the topic back to the ex as opposed to how much money she herself is spending) "He is such a good-for-nothing, and here I am raising HIS children! And I have to be working a full-time job!"

Me: "His children? Aren't they yours as well?"

Caroline: (Quickly adopting the appropriate motherly air) "Of course they are! I do everything for them, and I get no thanks from him or them!"

Me: "How often do you eat out?"

Caroline: (Adopting the victim face and tone) "Every day! I don't have time to cook! I'm a single mother! No one gets that I have no time! I have it harder than any other single mother. I have no family support, no friends, and now

YOU are turning on me!"

Me: (In my head) "Oh fuck. Here we go again."

The rest of the session was spent helping her see the victim language and victim story she told herself. The client would show some change for a session or two and then fall right back into victim mode, each time blaming the ex and the kids and basically anything and everyone around her for everything from her weight to her financial situation to the fact that she had no friends, or that the friends she had all used her. Eventually, I referred her to a Dialectic Behavioral Therapy (DBT) program as it was clear she was not making any progress doing Cognitive Behavioral Therapy (CBT). I do not believe she ever went as I never received a request for records.

Here is something to keep in mind: Abusers therapist shop. When someone tells me they have seen multiple therapists, and it wasn't because they had moved, I know they are therapist shopping. In other words, they are looking for a therapist who will support their dysfunctional behavior and abuse, as opposed to working on the dysfunctional behavior and abuse. Once the therapist starts holding them accountable, they will either stop coming to therapy or they will not do the homework or take suggestions. They would rather sit in a session and blame everyone around them and complain as oppose to grow and change. To allow them to do that for more than a session or two is a disservice to them and to the profession. Why do they do that? Because abusers are all about control. *(https://www. psychologytoday.com/blog/finding-your-voice/201207/control- resistance)*

Covert narcissists often play the martyr. They have some similarities to the Grandiose narcissists in that they consider themselves special and unique; however, it is usually played from the victim role. Make no mistake. If Caroline does not get this handled, she will eventually become grandiose and then malignant. Her teenage daughters were already spending as much time as they could with their father, whom the client bad-mouthed in front of them. *(https:// www.psychologytoday.com/ blog/communication-success/201601/7-signs-covert-introvert-narcissist)*

Here is a clear example of the martyr role narcissists play. Again all names and identifying characteristics have been changed.

Ted, age 72. Recently divorced. Alcoholic.

Me: "Hey Ted. What are we working on today?"

Ted: (Angry) "Hey asshole!"

Me: "Excuse me?"

Ted: "You're the reason I'm divorced!"

Me: "No, you are divorced because your wife filed for divorce." (I had seen them as a couple once before she filed for divorce and then separately after the divorce.)

Ted: (Dismissively) "Whatever."

Me: "So what do you want to work on?"

Ted: "I'm lonely." (He began to tear up.)

Me: "I thought you were dating and painting the town red?"

Ted: (Quickly losing the tears and getting angry again) "I was until I found out Tina is living with my son and his wife and kids!"

Me: "You are lonely because your ex is living with your son and daughter-in-law?"

Ted: "They didn't ask me to live with them! They asked HER to live with them! I should be living with them after all I've done for them!"

Me: "But you have your own place that you bought after the divorce. My understanding from you was that the house had to be sold and Tina had nowhere else to go."

Ted: (Again, dismissive when the truth is brought up) "They should have asked me!" (Switching gears) "I am so mad at Tina for divorcing me!"

Me: "But you were the one talking about divorcing her."

Ted: "Yes! But she divorced me! How dare she?"

Me: (Inside my head) "Ah, now we get to what the real issue is. It isn't that he is divorced; it is that she beat him to the punch." (Outside my head) "Ted, it is what it is."

Ted: "But my son is letting her live with him!" (As if I should take his side and start damning the son for helping his own mother)

Me: "So why are you letting that bother you so much?"

Ted: "Because she is there! I can't just go over there because I don't want to run into her!"

Me: "So just call your son and meet him or the grandkids somewhere else."

Ted: "Yes, but he is MY son! And those are MY grandkids! Why should I go somewhere else? I can't believe she divorced me!"

Me: (Inside my head) "Say what, homie?" (Outside my head) "Ted, you told me how unhappy you were with your marriage. How much you wanted to be out of it."

Ted: "Yes, but SHE filed for divorce!"

And so it went. "Yes, buts..." for the entire session. It was clear his ego was butt hurt that she had filed first and that she so obviously did not miss him at all. His ego wanted her to be homeless and for the family to reject her. When he did run into her, he would put on the mask of how much he missed her. But in the session he would state over and over how happy he was to be divorced. He wanted her to miss him, but he had no intention of going back into the relationship. He played the ultimate victim to family and friends, wearing whatever mask he deemed necessary to get his narcissistic supply.

Next, let's take a look at the Somatic narcissist. A Somatic narcissist is all about physical appearance. Again, all names and identifying characteristics have been changed.

Tom, age 60, actor, former model, divorced, thin, fit, tanned. Always dressed to the nines. Very good-looking but in a very plastic kind of way.

Me: "Good morning, Tom! What would you like to focus on today?"

Tom: (Starting to tear up) "She left me for a younger man!"

Me: "Sarah?" (He had been playing sugar daddy to a very beautiful 26-year-old woman.)

Tom: "Yes! She left me for a 26-year-old! I am looking too old! I am going to get more hair plugs and have my face lifted again."

Me: (Thinking in my head "Dear God, you already have beard stubble on the back of your neck from all the facelifts he had already had!") "Tom, you don't need surgery. It may not be because of age or looks; it may be because she needed someone closer to her own age who could relate to her well."

Tom: "You think I look old and hideous, don't you?"

Me: "No, I most certainly do not. I think you look amazing."

Tom: "For my age."

Me: (Sighing, he was clearly fishing for reassurance and compliments) "Tom, every time you have a relationship end you go and have plastic surgery done. How many surgeries have you had?"

Tom: "10. And I am going to fight aging tooth and nail with every dollar I have! It's not fair! It's not fair that everyone is younger and more handsome than I am!"

Me: (Again in my head) "Hmm. Interesting. The client had mentioned being jealous of his own son's youth and looks. I was not surprised to hear that the son no longer had contact with the client." (Outside of my head) "Well, Tom, the only things guaranteed in life are death and taxes."

Tom: (Wailing.) "I don't want to get old! I don't want to die!"

We spent the rest of the session dealing with his fear of death and aging, not necessarily in that order. Show me a narcissist, whether it be a Somatic one, a Grandiose one, or a Covert one, and I will show you someone terrified of death and aging. Why are they all so terrified to age and die? Probably because they have absolutely no control over the event, and no matter how much they manipulate and control and have plastic surgeries, they will eventually die, like the rest of us mortals. *(http:// flyingmonkeysdenied.com/2016/02/24/somatic-narcissists- are-obsessed-with-appearance-and-status/)* Also remember narcissists—whether Grandiose, Covert, or Somatic—all operate on no more than the emotional level of a six-year-old. *(https://*

www.psychologytoday.com/blog/the-career-within-you/201609/the-child-s-fear-death)

Let me give another example of a Somatic narcissist.

Gina, age 75. Widowed. No support system. Coming in for anxiety and depressed mood. Came in with heavy makeup and clothes, which were not becoming to her because they were too tight and made for someone much younger. She was morbidly obese.

Me: "Hey Gina! How can I help you today?"

Gina: "My family has stopped talking to me."

Me: (In my head) "Whoa! Red Flag!" (Outside my head) "What do you mean they've stopped talking to you?"

Gina: "They are angry because I like to have boyfriends."

Me: (Sensing that there was way more to the story than she was telling at this point) "Ok. So why does that bother them?"

Gina: "They think I am being ridiculous! They think I should act my age!"

Me: "I noticed you left your birth date and age off of the intake form. What is your age?"

Gina: (Squirming, I could tell she considered lying to me before she finally said) "I'm 75." (Then she yelled) "I DON'T WANT TO BE 75!! I like to date men much younger than me because I feel much younger than 75!!"

Me: "So why does your family care who you date?"

Gina: "Because they think the men I get involved with take advantage of me! I just broke up with Johnny, he was 32. I am all alone, and I feel so frightened!"

Me: "So if you just broke up with him, why is your family not speaking to you?"

Gina: (Pressured speech) "I need to be talking to someone all the time! I HATE being alone! I HATE IT!!!! If I can't get them on the phone to talk, I text."

Me: "Who in your family are you trying to talk to?"

Gina: "My four children. Three sons and a girl. I haven't spoken to my daughter in over three years! She refuses my texts and phone calls."

Me: "How often do you text or call?"

Gina: "Every day."

Me: "How often every day?

Gina: "Hundreds of times a day."

Me: (Inside my head) "Hundreds? Jesus Christ, no wonder they are pissed!" (Outside my head) "Gina, how old are your children?"

Gina: "They are in their 40s. They should make time for me! They should answer my calls and texts! Instead, they blocked all of my numbers that I call or text them from! Is that legal?"

Me: "I am assuming they have jobs and kids of their own? And what do you mean ALL of your phone numbers?"

Gina: "Yes. They all have jobs and kids. Every time they block my number, I get a new number and try to call them or text them!"

Me: (Recognizing she had absolutely no insight as to why they blocked her) "Gina, it is legal to block numbers, and when someone does that, it means they are feeling harassed."

Gina: (Wailing) "I want them to pay attention to ME! I am so alone and frightened!"

Me: "Tell me about your living situation." (Trying to determine if she was homeless)

Gina: "I live in a condo but it is being sold so I have to move in two months."

Me: "Maybe it would be good to move into a 55 or older place or move to an assisted living facility where you will have companionship."

Gina: (Angry) "I want nothing to do with old people!! I am NOT old! I don't want to be 75! I want to be surrounded by youth and beauty!"

Me: "Gina, whether you want to be 75 or not, you are. It looks like you are having health issues, and it would be good for you to be safe and in an environment where you can be looked in on."

Gina: (Wailing) "My doctor told me I was morbidly obese! How dare he! When I hear the word morbid, I think of grotesque and horrid and OLD!!"

Me: (In my head) "Oh boy. Here we go!" (Outside my head) "Morbid meaning deadly. You are deadly obese. Your weight is going to kill you if you don't do something about it." (On her intake she listed several high blood pressure and diabetes medications.)

Gina: (Now absolutely inconsolable) "I don't want to die!"

Me: "Then you are going to have to change your eating

habits and start exercising and follow what your doctor recommended."

Gina: "I can't! I'm all alone! My family should be helping me! Why aren't they returning my phone calls? Why? Why did they block me?"

This woman was morbidly obese, could barely walk, most definitely looked her age no matter how much makeup she caked on, and had absolutely no insight into why her family had stopped speaking to her. She honestly thought that the gold diggers she picked up were interested in her as a sex object, as opposed to only being interested in her Social Security check. Because she had absolutely no insight into the fact that her behavior was the problem, she continued to be taken advantage of by unscrupulous young men so her family steadfastly had disowned her. I got Adult Protective Services involved but, because she was an adult and not a danger to herself or anyone else, they could not help her. She was terrified of aging. She was terrified of dying. She could not stand the thoughts in her head, and that was why she desperately needed to be distracted either by lovers or by her family and when lovers were unavailable she would harass her family. She absolutely refused to believe that her family disowned her because of her obsessive calling and texting, and she could not own up to anything she had ever done or said that would cause them to quit talking to her. In her mind, it was all them. They were the problem—even for her being morbidly obese. That was all their fault, too.

These two Somatic narcissists were older. Younger ones are found all over social media and especially on online dating sites. *(https://www.psychologytoday.com/blog/media-spotlight/201611/updated-snapshot-the-online-narcissist)* All you have to do is look for someone who posts nothing but selfies—especially selfies done in the bathroom mirror where they make the infamous duck lips or pouty face. *(https://www.psychologytoday.com/blog/why-bad-looks-good/201705/online-dating-photo-*

fraud-the-person-behind-the-profile) This goes for both male and female Somatic narcissists. *(https://www.psychologytoday. com/blog/close-proximity/201706/are-you-self-ie-absorbed)*

However, narcissists are not the only type of personality disorder that abuses others.

"I'm so good at the beginnings,
but, in the end, I always seem to destroy everything.
Including myself."

Kiera Van Gelder

THE ABUSERS WHO ARE BORDERLINES

Alright. So what about abusers with Borderline Personality Disorder. They, too, have different types: The Queen, The Witch, The Hermit, and The Waif, which, if put into layman's terms, translates as The Controller (Machiavellian), The Sadist (psychopath), The Anxiety-Ridden (fear), and The Victim (helpless). Again, I will use case studies to illustrate and again, all names and identifying details have been changed.

First, let's start with the definition from the DSM-5.

"A pervasive pattern of instability of interpersonal relationships, self-image, and affects and marked impulsivity, beginning by early adulthood and present in a variety of contexts as indicated by five or more of the following:

1. Frantic efforts to avoid real or imagined abandonment.

2. A pattern of unstable and intense interpersonal relationships characterized by alternating extremes of idealization and devaluation.

3. Identity disturbance: markedly and persistently unstable self-image or sense of self.

4. Impulsivity in at least two areas that are potentially self-damaging (e.g., spending, sex, substance abuse, reckless driving, binge eating).

5. Recurrent suicidal behavior, gestures, or threats, or self-mutilating behavior.

6. Affective instability due to a marked reactivity of mood

(e.g., intense episodic dysphoria, irritability, or anxiety usually lasting a few hours and only rarely more than a few days).

7. Chronic feelings of emptiness.

8. Inappropriate, intense anger or difficulty controlling anger (e.g., frequent displays of temper, constant anger, recurrent physical fights).

9. Transient, stress-related paranoid ideation or severe dissociative symptoms.

Borderline has traits of all 10 major personality disorders and borders on Talionic *(eye for an eye) or psychotic thinking. (http:// ajmahari.ca/2014/09/why-people-with-borderline-personality-and-punishment/)*

Let's take a look at a malignant borderline with The Queen attributes, which, you will notice, are remarkably similar to the NPD Grandiose type. *(https://www.psychologytoday.com / articles/201309/kings-and-queens-chaos)*

Again, all identifying traits and names have been changed.

Ann is a 55-year-old female, overweight with thinning brown hair pulled back in a bun. She has come to therapy only because her spouse has asked for a divorce so Ann demanded they go to therapy. When she had called and wanted to know if I would tell them to get divorced, I had answered, "No. I don't tell clients what to do. I let them come to their own decisions." Satisfied with that answer, she made the appointment.

Ben, her spouse, is age 54, tall, and good-looking, but he has dark circles under his eyes and looks haggard. They arrive at my office in separate cars.

Me: "Hi. So how can I help you two?"

Ann: (Not even allowing Ben a word, not even looking at him) "We are here to save our marriage!"

Me: "How long have you been married?"

Ann: "30 years." (Again, not letting Ben answer)

Me: "Do you have children?"

Ann: "Two boys, who are 20 and 21 years old. Ben moved out two weeks ago."

Ben: "I filed for divorce. I do not want to be here."

Me: "Ah. Okay, so on a scale of one to ten, how interested are you in saving this marriage?" (I ask this question to all my couples to make sure everyone is on the same page.)

Ann: (Almost before I get the question out of my mouth) "10! Definitely a 10!"

Ben: (Rolling his eyes) "1." (Long pause.) "1 and a half at the most. I want a divorce."

Ann: (Clearly ignoring what he just said) "1 and a half! That's great! Our marriage can be saved! I thought you were going to say zero! You need to move back in this afternoon!"

Me: "Whoa! Hold on, there. Ben, let me be sure I heard you and that Ann hears you. On a scale of 1 to 10 for saving the marriage, you are at a 1, maybe a 1 and a half, and you really want a divorce."

Ann: (Starting to interrupt) "NO! He said 1 and a half so that means he wants to move back…"

Me: (Cutting her off) "Ann, I need you to let Ben answer."

Ann: (Now glaring at me like she would physically kill me if she could)

Ben: (Looking happy to have someone stand up for him) "I do not want to be married to her anymore! I'm done. I'm done being bullied and bossed and put down! 1! 1 and a half at most! I want a damn divorce!"

Me: "Okay, well, then, the conversation needs to change to how to separate amicably then."

Ann: (Screaming) "NO! NO!" (Turning and looking at Ben for the first time) "YOU WILL STAY MARRIED TO ME! You divorce me, and I WILL make your life a living hell!! I WILL take EVERYTHING you own!"

Me: (Recognizing I am dealing with a malignant BPD) "Actually, Ann, the state of Arizona is very loathe to do that. Usually, it is pretty much split up the middle. The kids are grown so there will be no child support or custody issues."

Ann: (Now wanting revenge on Ben for refusing to reconcile) "I want alimony! You WILL be paying me for the next 20 years if you leave me! The judge will give me at least $5,000 a month!"

Me: (Thinking in my head) "Wow! This chick is out of her ever-loving gourd if she thinks she is getting alimony, let alone that much." (Outside of my head) "Ok, so that is for the lawyers and judges to decide. Ann, do you work?"

Ann: (Snarling) "He is incompetent! I have to work to make enough money for us."

Ben: (Showing emotion for the first time) "Ann, I am getting really sick of your bullshit! I work full time and always have and provided nicely for us and the kids. You have worked the whole time we have been married. I am not paying you one damn red cent of alimony!"

Ann: (Attacking me, shrieking.) "YOU! You said you wouldn't tell us to get divorced!"

Me: "I didn't."

Ann: (Clearly rewriting history) "You said you would save our marriage!"

Me: (Staying calm) "No. I never said that. I cannot guarantee the outcome of any therapy. Nor did I ever imply I would save your marriage."

Ben: (Sighing.) "Ann, I cannot stand you. I hate you. You put me down, you never give me a moment's peace. I have no friends because of you, and I am tired of your shit. I am done. I'm sick of your abuse, and so are the kids. I want a divorce, and I am going to get a divorce."

Ann: (Turning on me) "This is all your fault! You are just like all the other therapists we've seen!"

Me: (Amused but not showing it, knowing that malignant BPDs therapist shop, looking for a therapist that will validate their world view.) "How many therapists have you been to?"

Ann: "Eight! They all blame me! Like I'm the problem!"

Ben: (Shaking his head) "You ARE the problem, Ann. I'm done. I want a divorce!"

Me: (Jumping in before Ann has a chance to start screaming again) "Well, I think Ben has made it clear that therapy will not repair this marriage. In order for therapy to work, the clients have to be both at a 5 or above, and Ben has stated several times he does not want to fix this relationship."

Ann: (Screaming) YOU LIED TO ME!!! YOU SAID YOU WOULDN'T TELL US TO DIVORCE!"

Me: (Calm as a cucumber) "Ann, I never said that to you. Your relationship, according to Ben, is over. I would suggest seeking legal counsel, both of you."

Ben: (Handing me payment) "Thank you."

Ann: (Glaring at me all the way out the door; if looks could kill I would have been a puddle of yuck on the floor if she had her way.)

Two hours later I received a phone call from Ann in which she raged, screaming incoherently at times, stating that I was to blame for her marriage dissolving. I listened and said, "I am truly sorry you feel that way." And I refused to rise to her bait. She screamed that she would file a complaint with my state board, and I told her that was her right to do so. She continued to scream for another few minutes, and when I wouldn't play her game, she called me several nasty names, threatened again to go to the board, and then hung up. Nothing ever came of her threats. Borderlines like this are about control and power, and in this case, Ann had neither. She could neither manipulate nor intimidate me, and she could not dissuade Ben from divorcing her.

Ben sought individual therapy with me. Ann was so controlling that she told Ben what to wear, what to eat, what to like, etc. If he or the children ever had an opinion of their own, Ann would browbeat them until they agreed with her. She treated dissention with her as a form of high treason and worthy of verbal and sometime physical punishment. The kids moved out of the house as soon as they could and wanted no contact with her.

Ann attempted to use the courts to force Ben to pay both literally and figuratively. She wanted revenge, not justice, and she wanted more than what was reasonable, which is not surprising. *(https://www.psychologytoday.com/blog/evolution-the-self/201402/don-*

t-confuse-revenge-justice-five-key-differences) The judge saw through the games, but even at that, the divorce dragged out well over a year due to her constantly filing motions including a demand for conciliation, which Ben refused to attend. All of the motions were denied, and most of them were around punishing Ben by trying to take all of his money and possessions, even though she had worked and held jobs their entire marriage. Ann also barraged the judge with a series of letters, painting herself as a saint and Ben as the devil. In the end she got nothing. However, she did everything she could to fulfill her promise to make Ben's life a living, flaming hell.

"Why would someone do that?" you ask. Borderlines, but particularly malignant borderlines and particularly Machiavellian Queen types, cannot tolerate being abandoned or losing. The divorce in Ann's mind was an affront to her ego. She knew best! It wasn't about the dissolution of a 30-year marriage, it wasn't the loss of a love, or the loss of her best friend, it was "How DARE you defy me and leave me! How DARE you not allow me to control you!" She was going to seek revenge any way she could.

When trying to intimidate through using legal avenues did not pan out, she began texting and emailing and stalking on social media and showing up at his apartment and work. (https:// www .psychologytoday.com/blog/in-excess/201410/look-whos-stalking) She even went so far as to contact his HR people in an attempt to get him fired and, of course, sent a 14-page letter detailing their life together and how he should be fired for leaving her. The world view through the eyes of both malignant borderlines and malignant narcissists is one of competition. They must win at all costs—and I do mean at all costs. This behavior is known as not only stalker behavior but Obsessive Ex Syndrome. *(http://flyingmonkeysdenied.com/2016/06/09/what-is-obsessive-ex-syndrome-or-vendetta-stalking/)*

Any form of stalking should be taken very seriously. Stalkers almost always have a personality disorder and are dangerous. *(https://www.psychologytoday.com/blog/tech-support/201707 / the-psychology-revenge-and-vengeful-people)* They will stop only when it is obvious that their behavior will hurt them and sometimes not even then, if they are psychotic enough in their obsession. Obsessive stalkers will do things such as steal passwords, read and forward private emails ,texts, and instant messages, intercept snail mail, vandalize homes and cars, put key stroke loggers onto computers, and put spyware on phones and tracking apps, etc. I always advise my clients once they leave an abuser and the ex is engaging in stalker behavior to get rid of the current phone and computer. If they can't, I put their phones in a drawer in the waiting room when they come in for therapy, as stalkers have been known to install apps that can turn on the microphone so they can listen in and spy on their object of obsession. *(https://victims ofcrime.org/our-programs/stalking-resource-center/help-for-victims/stalking-safety-planning)*

Next, let's take a look at The Witch type. Again, all identifying characteristics and names have been changed.

Lori, age 30, is a tall, unattractive, mannish appearing woman, slightly overweight with short black hair. Her facial expression is one of dissatisfaction even when she is not speaking.

Sebastian, age 30, is her spouse. Tall, athletic, handsome, blond-haired, and good-looking, his facial expression is one of kindness, even when not speaking.

They have sought marriage counseling due to distance in the relationship and dissatisfaction on the part of Sebastian.

Me: "Hi. What are we working on today?"

Sebastian: "We need to work on communication. Lori and I have been drifting apart for months."

Lori: (Looking bored with the situation; no real interest or change in expression)

Me: "Ok. How long have you been married?"

Sebastian: "6 years. We have two adorable girls. Natalie, who is 5, and Charlotte, who is 2."

Lori: (With contempt) "He doesn't pay enough attention to me!"

Sebastian: (Looking exasperated) "Lori, we work together. I pay attention to you all day." (Looking at me) "We have our own business, and we work from home so we are home with the kids as well."

Lori: "I am so stressed out. I have a nanny help me with the kids."

Me: "Ok. So when did you guys start having problems?"

Lori: (Starting to perk up and getting a nasty glint in her eye) "Five years ago when we had our first child. Superman here can't get it up anymore. Can you?"

Sebastian: (Looking abashed) "Lori,..."

Lori: (Now on a roll) "You can't perform in bed! You couldn't get it up if your life depended on it! You are pathetic. I'm sorry I ever married you!"

Me: (Stopping her) "Okay. Scale of 1 to 10, how interested are you guys in saving the marriage?"

Lori: "Oh! A 10!"

Sebastian: (Looking as surprised as I was) "A 5."

Lori: (Again, with contempt) "Of course, you aren't committed."

Me: "Obviously, there is some anger and resentment here. Tell me about how you communicate."

Sebastian: "We don't. Lately, all Lori wants to do is go hang out with her girlfriends and party. I take care of the children more than she does."

Lori: (Defensive) "Why should I? I carried them for nine months! You don't love me! If you loved me you wouldn't complain about how much money I spend! You would trust me! You wouldn't have someone else looking at the books!"

Sebastian: (Looking at me) "There are some discrepancies that I cannot account for with our business so I hired an outside CPA to go over the books."

Lori: "I just want to have fun! I don't want to be a mother anymore!"

Sebastian: (Disgusted) "A little late for that, don't you think?"

Lori: "Everyone knows I didn't want to be a mother! It's all your fault."

Me: "I do believe it takes two people to make a baby. Did you not discuss this before you got married?"

Lori: (Getting irritated) "I don't mind the younger one but the older one wants me to play with her all the time! I don't have time for that! I want to go do stuff for me!"

Sebastian: "She told Natalie she would rather be with her girlfriends than her and then laughed when Natalie cried."

Me: (Looking at Sebastian) "And what did you do?"

Sebastian: "Comforted Natalie, took the kids, and went to my parents' house."

Lori came to one more session in which it was crystal clear she enjoyed humiliating both her husband and verbally abusing her children. At one point, she stated that she sat the kids and Sebastian down, raged at them, and told them she loved her horse more than them and would rather be at the bar drinking. She was absolutely impervious to the hurt she caused the entire family; she was proud of what she had done, and it clearly pleased her to see her children cry and even better if she could make her spouse cry. When she said something hurtful in that session, it was with a sadistically satisfied smirk on her face. When I let her know that intentionally harming her family emotionally was in no way, shape, or form okay, she quit coming to therapy, which was good because I wasn't about to continue to do couples counseling with an obvious abuser. According to Sebastian, she would tell employees, total strangers out in public, and anyone else who would listen what a "loser" he was, how he couldn't please her in bed, and how he didn't give her enough attention or money. She was sadistic and cruel and enjoyed it. She began having an affair with a neighbor on her street and was flaunting it, almost as if she was daring Sebastian to say or do anything about it. To his credit, he did. He divorced her and got the kids into therapy. Turned out she had been embezzling from their business to pay for a boob job, which she justified by saying, "He owed it to me!" She later was arrested for extreme intoxication with the children in the car during one of her days with the kids. Thankfully, the kids were okay, and Sebastian was granted temporary full custody.

Sebastian stayed in therapy for about a year and a half after that, and we worked on his self-esteem. He definitely had Complex Post-Traumatic Stress Disorder (CPTSD), which is slightly different than PTSD in that the trauma is repeated over and over and over again by the abuser with emotional abuse *(https:// www.psychologytoday.com/blog/the-aftermath-trauma/201410/ the-complexities-diagnosing-ptsd)*, and we had to work to undo the damage that Lori had done. Sebastian was smart in that he stayed in therapy and stayed single to work on himself. He knew that if he wasn't okay, the kids were not going to be okay and that he had no business getting into another relationship until he was in a healthy relationship with himself.

People with BPD who are sadistic as The Witch type take great pleasure in harming their spouse, their kids, and anyone else they can put down or insult. Although Sadistic Personality Disorder was dropped from the DSM-5, it is definitely a part of the BPD with The Witch type. *(https:// www.psychologytoday. com/blog/sideways-view/201612/sadistic-personality-disorder)* It is all about power and control. They cannot emotionally regulate or accept responsibility for their own actions and choices, much like their counterparts with NPD.

Next, let's look at The Hermit type. The Hermit type is filled with anxiety. They are more inclined to hurt themselves than someone else. They tend to isolate and push people away, almost in a misguided power play of "I will leave them before they can leave me!" game.

Again, identifying characteristics and names have been changed.

Sarah, age 20, is petite, of average weight, and waifish in appearance.

Connor, her boyfriend, is also age 20, slightly taller than Sarah, and of average weight.

Me: "Hi! What do you want to work on today?"

Sarah: "Connor doesn't know how to handle disagreements."

Connor: "When I get angry I tell her I want to break up with her."

Sarah: (Very concerned) "Last Thursday after we had an

argument, he locked himself in the bathroom and cut on himself."

Me: (Also concerned) "Connor?"

Connor: "I told Sarah I wanted to break up with her, but I don't really want to break up with her. I just feel so much, and I don't know what to do so I cut myself and then I feel better."

Me: "Okay. So let me reflect back what I am hearing. When confronted with disagreements or arguments, you push Sarah away so that she cannot hurt you first. Then you have so much emotion or anxiety that you don't know what to do with it so cutting helps you relieve the stress. Did I get that right?" *(https://www.psychologytoday.com/ blog/overcoming-self-sabotage/201001/cutting-escape-emotional-pain)*

Connor: (Looking relieved) "Yes! Exactly!"

Sarah: (Holding his hand) "That isn't fair to me, Connor, or to you."

Connor: (Looking ashamed) "I know. I just don't know how else to cope."

I worked with this couple and taught them reflective listening and other communication skills. I also worked individually with Connor and taught him stress coping skills over the course of a year. Connor's family of origin was chaotic. His mom and dad fought constantly, and he started cutting to ease his fear and stress when they went through a divorce when he was age 10. He felt the need to be "in control" of the situation and would push people away if he felt they were about to leave, just like he did with his own father, but once he pushed them away the fear of permanent abandonment kicked in. Then Connor would cut to ease his anxiety, just like he did when he was a child. Connor's knee-jerk reaction was to push away; however, he was eventually able to regulate the emotions and the anxiety and stay in the present moment to deal with the disagreement with Sarah. Sarah called him on his behavior if he attempted to push her away, and the two were able to maintain a mostly healthy relationship as long as Connor continued to work on himself and held himself accountable for his own feelings. He put together his own safety plan, which allowed him to feel in control of his life. At the last session he had not cut on himself for over six months, and they were planning to get married.

When The Hermit type goes malignant, they use the cutting behavior as a way to control their partner through the threat of self-harm. The more out of control an abuser is, the more they attempt to control people around them. *(https://www. psychologytoday.com/blog/intimacy-and-desire/201105/people- who-cant-control-themselves-control-the-people-around-them)*

 Let's look at an example. Again, all names and identifying characteristics have been changed.

Kylie, age 22, just out of college and working as a waitress.

Dustin, also age 22, is a waiter.

Me: "Hey guys! How can I help you?"

Kylie: (Looking very nervous) "I dunno. We just are fighting a lot."

Dustin: "We work at a restaurant together, and I don't like the way the guys flirt with her."

Kylie: "Dustin! That is how I get tips! You flirt with the old snowbirds."

Dustin: "Yeah, but I have no intention of sleeping with any of them!"

Kylie: "And you think I do?"

Me: (Interrupting) "Okay. Well, I see that we need to work on some communication skills."

Dustin: (Not allowing me to direct the session and continuing the argument with Kylie, relishing having an audience to play to) "Yeah, I do think you want to sleep with them!"

Kylie: (Getting more upset) "That is just ridiculous! I have never slept with any of the customers!"

Dustin: "I went through your phone, Kylie! You were talking to Philip!"

Kylie: (Now on the defensive) "Philip is an old friend from high school."

Dustin: (Now doing the preemptive abandonment) "That's it! I don't want this relationship! I want you to move out!"

Me: "Whoa! Full stop! How long have you guys been going out? How long have you been living together?"

Kylie: "We met six months ago and moved in together five months ago."

Me: "That is kind of quick, don't you think?"

Dustin: "I knew it was love at first sight! Why wait?"

Kylie: "Dustin wanted me to move in right away. I wanted to wait. Whenever we have a disagreement he threatens to hurt himself or tells me to move out, or both!"

Dustin: 'I wouldn't do it if you weren't flirting all the time! (Changing to pleading, recognizing his anger wasn't working) Baby, I just love you so much! That's why I'm jealous!"

Me: "Dustin, true love NEVER involves jealousy. Ever. What jealousy speaks to is massive insecurity and low self-esteem. Tell me about your mom and dad."

Dustin: (Annoyed that I didn't agree with him but continued to tell me about his family) "My mom and dad are divorced. I lived with my mom. She hated my dad. My mom lived with her boyfriends."

Me: "Boyfriends?"

Dustin: "Yeah. She could never keep one in her life very long, always screaming and fighting and arguments."

Me: "Kylie, how was your home life?"

Kylie: "Mom and Dad are divorced. Mom is an alcoholic. She and I fight all the time. Dad is out of the picture."

Dustin: "Her dad cheated on her mom all the time! Kylie is always flirting with her customers!"

These two had no healthy role models on how to have a healthy relationship. Dustin was showing strong traits of BPD. I suspected that Kylie, too, had strong traits of BPD. This was confirmed in the next exchange.

Kylie: "I flirt to make sure I get a tip. You are about to get fired, Dustin, if you keep threatening my customers every time I flirt with them."

Kylie then launched into the drama of being a waiter at the restaurant, and it became clear that she, too, was addicted to drama and had strong traits of BPD.

Me: "Alright. So you both need to be able to set boundaries and learn how to speak to each other respectfully."

The session ended. The next day I received a frantic phone call from Kylie.

Me: "Aha Counseling. This is Kris. How can I help you?"

Kylie: (Sobbing) "Dustin screamed at me all night, and he's threatening to kill himself!"

Me: "Are you safe? Where is he?"

Kylie: "I'm locked in our bedroom, but he's trying to break the door down. And he says if I don't open the door, he will cut himself and kill himself."

Me: "Kylie (grabbing my other phone and calling 911), I'm sending the police to your house."

Kylie: "NO! No! Don't do that!"

I did. What people don't listen to in my preamble during the first appointment is that I am a state mandated reporter, and if there is danger to self or others, I am obligated to report it. The police came and took him away for an involuntary 72-hour hold. Kylie came into session and told me that he had been screaming at her all night, threatening to kill himself because he was enraged that she was flirting with a customer. After he was released from the hold, I refused to see them as a couple and saw them both individually. He continued to attempt to use the threat of self-harm to keep Kylie from leaving him. He only came to individual therapy two more times, both times attempting to get messages to Kylie about how he would hurt himself. He was clearly addicted to the drama of the relationship. If he could not create drama with her, he attempted to create drama at their job and was eventually fired. He stopped coming to therapy when he realized he could not manipulate. Kylie, too, saw me for individual therapy. It became clear she was addicted to the drama as well, and it took her a few more months of therapy before she was finally able to move out and leave him for good. Unfortunately, she returned to her mother's house, where her mother continued to abuse her both physically and verbally. Her mother, too, would use the threat of self-harm to keep Kylie under her thumb. Kylie continued counseling off and on for the next few months. At last contact, she was still living a drama-filled life with her mother.

Something that is not often discussed is why it is so hard to treat someone with BPD. It is because of the family of origin. Often when someone with BPD does get help and does start making positive changes, the family tries to force them back into the drama and maladaptive behavior. (https://www.psychologytoday. com/blog/matter-personality/201506/why-patients-borderline-personality-dont-get-better) Parents, siblings, and others are still in the throes of maladaptive behavior, especially if they, too, have BPD do not want to see someone succeed where they have failed and will actively sabotage and prevent the person with BPD from getting help. That also explains why abusers with BPD will then sabotage and prevent their target from getting help. It is a learned behavior. *(https://www.psychologytoday.com/ blog/the-athletes-way/201605/neuroscience-pinpoints-how-the-brain-makes-and-breaks-habits)*

What do I mean when I say both the abuser and the abused were addicted to the drama? *(https://www.psychologytoday. com/blog/obesely-speaking/201411/excessive-attention-seeking-and-drama-addiction)* Well, the angst, the pathos, the fear, the intermittent positive rewards—they all release the same chemicals in the brain that meth, heroin, and alcohol do, which is the almighty serotonin, endorphins, dopamine, and norepinephrine that flood the system and give us a high. These two kids learned, from watching their dysfunctional families, how to behave in a relationship; the more drama, the more "exciting" it was until, of course, no one would put up with their nonsense—employers included.

Sometimes people stay in an abusive situation because to leave would feel like an anticlimax, boring, blah, passionless. I hear the same stories from my substance-addicted clients. What they don't understand is that passion does not mean pain and calm is not boring but, because that is what they are used to, they don't understand the difference and crave the "excitement" of the abuse.

People get as addicted to their abuser as people get addicted to meth, and that is why quitting cold turkey and going no contact with an abuser is so very important as is getting into treatment with a good counselor and working on the initial wound that caused the need to be in an abusive relationship. It is also why it is so goddamn hard to leave an abusive relationship. Both Kylie and Dustin were acting out abuse from their family of origin, and neither had ever worked on that original wound, which caused them to seek out abuse to try to work through the original abuse. Of course, it never gets worked out so more wounds are piled on top, totally obfuscating the original wound.

Now let's look at The Waif type. Waif type BPD is mostly a lot of victim language and victim mentality on the part of the person with the disorder.

Again, all identifying traits and names have been changed.

Chloe is 35 years old, overweight, single, has 1 daughter (age 13), and raises rabbits to show and sell.

Me: "Hello, Chloe! What are you working on today?"

Chloe: "I need to make more money!"

Me: (Frowning) "Okay. I thought you sold prized rabbits?"

Chloe: "Oh! Yes! I do! But, well, I would but I just can't stand the idea of them going to a home where they won't be appreciated."

Me: "So how many rabbits do you have right now?"

Chloe: "17."

Me: "And you aren't selling them."

Chloe: "No! Yes, but it isn't my fault."

Me: (Raising my eyebrow) "Um…"

Chloe: (Changing the topic and throwing in some word salad) "The breeders and the judges are so biased, and most of the people don't treat the rabbits well so they would be better off with me. I think you would agree they are better off with me."

Me: "I thought you started raising rabbits as a way to make money."

Chloe: "Yes, but I don't want the rabbits going to a bad home so I have to keep them."

Me: "And didn't you used to do real estate before?"

Chloe: "Yes, but that agency I was working at was crooked and would steal sales from me, and the coworkers were mean and jealous. I would sit at my desk and just cry, and no one would even try to comfort me."

Me: "And before that you worked at a car dealership?"

Chloe: "Yes, but the people I worked with were horrible, and I didn't like the long hours. The boss was an ogre and made me feel uncomfortable. My family doesn't understand. I don't deserve to work these horrible jobs, and I have to work because I'm a single mom. I have to provide for my daughter, and teenagers are expensive. She is growing, and I have to buy new clothes for her every few months."

Me: "Ok, so why not just find people who you know want the rabbits and will care for them? Surely, they are out there. You could do an inspection of the home just like the Rescues do for dogs.

Chloe: "Yes. But…"

And on and on it went. Every suggestion was met with a "yes, but" response, every solution was met with another unending problem, and every reason she couldn't get ahead in life was always someone else's fault. With both The Waif type and Covert narcissists, every solution is responded to with a "yes, but…" followed by a victim story of why that solution wouldn't work. *(https://www.psychologytoday.com/blog/anger-in-the-age-entitlement/200905/the-line-between-victims-and-abusers)* The Waif type shares a lot of characteristics with the Covert narcissist. In fact, you will see that a lot of people with BPD share a lot of characteristics with the corresponding NPD types. "Why?" you ask. Because BPD has traits of all 10 major personality disorders; especially the ones who have slid into malignancy can express all 10 traits in one sitting. Like with malignant narcissists, everything is on a spectrum from traits of to flat out malignant. If the person with BPD does not seek help and does not work on the maladaptive behaviors, they, too, will slide down the spectrum into malignancy and psychotic thinking.

"The signs of sociopathy are usually there before we are abused; most of us just don't know enough to recognize them."

P. A. Speers

ANTI-SOCIAL PERSONALITY DISORDERED ABUSERS

Anti-social, psychopath, and sociopath are all describing the same set of abusive and abhorrent behaviors. I have had people argue with me on this, claiming they are all different. No. They are not. What is different is that the American Psychological Association (APA) and the American Counseling Association (ACA) are concerned with labeling and stigmatizing so the terms psychopath and sociopath are no longer used and have been replaced by Anti-Social Personality Disorder. *(https://www .elementsbehavioralhealth.com/mental-health/psychopathy-vs-antisocial-personality-disorder/)*

Here is the DSM-5 definition of Anti-Social Personality Disorder (ASPD):

A. A pervasive pattern of disregard for and violation of the rights of others, occurring since age 15 years, as indicated by three (or more) of the following:

1. Failure to conform to social norms with respect to lawful behaviors, as indicated by repeatedly performing acts that are grounds for arrest.

2. Deceitfulness, as indicated by repeated lying, use of aliases, or conning others for personal profit or pleasure.

3. Impulsivity or the failure to plan ahead.

4. Irritability and aggressiveness as indicated by repeated physical fights or assaults.

5. Reckless disregard for safety of self or others.

6. Consistent irresponsibility, as indicated by repeated failure to sustain consistent work behavior or honor financial obligations.

7. Lack of remorse as indicated by being indifferent to or rationalizing having hurt, mistreated, or stolen from another.

B. The individual is at least age 18 years.

C. There is evidence of conduct disorder with onset before age 15 years.

D. The occurrence of antisocial behavior is not exclusively during the course of schizophrenia or bipolar disorder.

You will notice as I give case studies that some behavior from the Cluster B—ASPD, borderline, narcissistic, histrionic—all seem very similar and share commonalities. In all likelihood histrionic personality disorder will be removed from the DSM-5 or blended into the borderline diagnosis, and there will be changes to the personality disorders section as no changes have been implemented in over 20 years. *(https://ct.counseling. org/2017/02/apa-welcome-dsm-feedback/)*

What I am concerned about is that the last time there was a revision to the DSM-5, there was a very large group of Humanist therapists that wanted to get rid of the personality disorder section altogether as they don't believe in "labeling." I believe that would be a huge mistake, dangerous, and a disservice to those who have been targeted. I will suggest here that if you have been a target of abuse by a personality disordered person, please contact both the APA and the ACA and voice that you do not want personality disorders removed from the DSM-5. *(http:// www.apa.org/membership/?keyword=apa&gclid=Cj0KCQj wktHLBRDsARIsAFBSb6wy-l7rTHTYLQ1RpatjPDm9fxQco_ nLeqsUExXO_Oj_OkOgdWZst50aAsrFEALw_wcB and https:// www.counseling.org/)*

Anti-social abusers are very dangerous because of their lack of remorse and their impulsiveness.

Again, all names and identifying characteristics have been changed in the following case studies.

Charles, age 50, very sweet-looking, brown hair. Presented with severe depression. Suicidal ideation. Multiple health issues. Middle child of three. Former kindergarten teacher, now retired due to health issues.

Me: "Hey Charles. What's up? What brings you in?"

Charles: "I want to die."

Me: "Do you have a plan?"

Charles: "No."

Me: "How serious are you about checking out of the planet?"

Charles: (Sobbing) "I'm not serious but I am just in so much pain."

Me: "Okay, so this is more an expression of the emotional pain you are in rather than really wanting to die?"

Charles: "Yes. I have seen doctor after doctor. My stomach is a mess. It hurts so bad all the time, and they can't find any reason."

Me: "Oh wow! That sounds terrible. (Now I need to rule out the client being a hypochondriac.) How long have you had stomach problems?"

Charles: "Ever since I was little."

Me: (Now suspecting he was abused) Tell me about your family and your childhood."

Charles: "They were okay, I guess."

It took months for him to tell me that he had been abused. At first, he said his family was "okay" so we worked on coping skills to deal with the physical pain and the depression. But then he finally started trusting me and opened up.

Me: "Hey Charles! What are we working on today?"

Charles: (Grabbing the tissue box and holding onto it for dear life) "I want to tell you about my brother and my mother."

Me: "Okay. I'm listening."

Charles: "My brother raped me repeatedly when I was a child, and my mother let him."

Me: (Because he had only focused on the physical issues as the cause of his anxiety and depression, I had diagnosed him with adjustment disorder with mixed anxiety and depressed mood. Now that he was telling the whole story, I recognized the need to change the diagnosis to CPTSD so this was a HUGE breakthrough for him) "Only tell me what you want to."

Charles: "I need to tell you everything if I'm going to get better!" (He began sobbing.)

Me: "It's okay to cry. Crying is cathartic. It just means we have been through something very painful. Every single mammal on the face of the planet tears up when they feel pain."

Charles: "This is the only place I feel safe in."

Me: (Nodding.) "I understand."

Charles: (Continuing) "My mother and father split when

I was 2, and my older brother, Don, was five years older than me. He was always hitting me every chance he could, but not like normal sibling rivalry type of thing. I mean my mother would have to stop him from killing me, like really."

Me: "What do you mean?"

Charles: "My earliest memory of him is when he was trying to smother me with a pillow, and my mother was screaming at him to stop."

Me: "Wow."

Charles: "He started molesting me when Mom went to work. She worked as a cocktail waitress so she would leave us alone in the house. Don was supposed to babysit me, but instead he took that opportunity to hurt me and touch me." (He began to uncontrollably shake and sob.)

Me: "Breathe. You are safe. You are okay. I am right here. He cannot hurt you anymore." (He was having a flashback as if he were experiencing the abuse. Flashbacks, reliving the trauma, are a hallmark symptom of CPTSD.)

Charles: (Catching his breath) "He would touch me and rub himself on me and then choke me or twist my arm until it hurt and say things like 'If you tell Mom I will kill you!'"

Me: (Out loud) "Holy shit! Charles, it is a testament to you that you are still here and functioning!"

Charles: (Smiling shyly but still crying) "Really?"

Me: "Yes. Really."

Charles: (Gathering courage and continuing) "My mother tried to drown me in the bathtub. She would hold me under, then pull me back up. I don't know if she was trying to kill me or what but she did that several times and tell me how much she hates me."

Me: "How old were you when this happened?"

Charles: "Little. Like maybe 3 or 4 years old. I don't know if she stopped Don from smothering me because she wanted to kill me or if she recognized that it was wrong. She is a horrible person, Kris! I hate her! She is living with my sister right now, and my sister is not doing well."

Me: "What's happening with your sister?"

Charles: "Melanie is bipolar, and my mother just pokes and pokes and pokes at her until she is near a nervous breakdown. My sister is single, and she feels obligated to take care of Mom."

Me: "How old is your mom?"

Charles: "75. She smokes at least three packs of cigarettes a day. Her doctor told her to stop smoking, but she won't, and Melanie has been trying to quit. But then Mom will smoke in front of her or demand that she smoke with her."

Me: "Wow."

Charles: "What I'm afraid of is that Melanie will not be able to keep her since she is nearing her breaking point and that I'll have to take her in."

Me: "Whoa! Hold the phone there! You are under NO obligation to take her in, you know that, right?"

Charles: "But she is my mom!"

Me: "You just said you hate her. You are still dealing with the fear, obligation, and guilt."

Charles: "I do feel guilty, but, but, she is my mom. I owe it to her to take care of her!"

Me: (Asking the million-dollar question when people feel obligated to care for an abusive family member) "If you were not related to her, would you have anything to do with her?"

Charles: "No. But she is my mom!"

Me: (Recognizing he wasn't ready to deal with his mom yet) "Tell me more about your brother Don."

Charles: "He was in trouble with the law most of his life. He would punish our dogs by hitting them or choking them if they pissed him off and then he would say they deserved it. (He shivered and continued.) He continued to sexually molest me for years. I remember him throwing me in the bathtub and plugging in the toaster and then dangling the toaster over the water. He said he would electrocute me and Mom wouldn't miss me at all. I think he was right about that. I think the only thing that stopped him was how would he explain me being electrocuted when he was supposed to be watching me. Eventually, I told him I was going to tell Mom what he was doing to me. So he dug a hole out in the field behind the house and, after raping me again, he dragged me out to the field, threw me in the hole, and started covering me in dirt."

Me: "Jesus! Charles, how did you get out of that?"

Charles: "One of the neighbors heard me screaming at him and walked over. I think the neighbor knew that I was being abused because she said something like "I'm watching you" to Don, and he never tried that again. I have a feeling that he eventually did kill."

Me: (Frowning) "What do you mean?"

Charles: "When he left home he bragged about seeing prostitutes and doing to them what he did to me, only (here he paused and gulped) successfully. I know I'm lucky I survived."

Me: "Hon, you did not deserve to be treated like that. No child does."

Charles: "My stomach hurts all the time. I have flashbacks to the abuse. I don't sleep. I feel exhausted all the time! I have nightmares when I do sleep."

Me: "Sweetie, you have severe CPTSD. Complex Post-Traumatic Stress Disorder. Slightly different than PTSD in that it was physical and emotional abuse that occurred over and over and over again for years rather than a one-time traumatic event. You aren't crazy. Your stomach hurts and doctors cannot find anything because your body is responding to the trauma of being repeatedly raped and almost killed. Your body is responding as if the abuse were still happening."

Charles: "You really think my physical illness is because of what I went through as a child?"

Me: "You are a survivor, Charles, and way stronger than you give yourself credit for. Yes. I think the CPTSD is what is making your stomach hurt and keeping you up at night."

Neither Don nor his mother ever had remorse for what they did to him, and when Melanie finally did have a mental breakdown, Charles took his mother in until the mother began verbally browbeating him. Fortunately, Charles was married to a very kind and strong woman who stood up to his mother. When the mother found that brow beating Charles didn't work, she changed tactics and decided to go for the public humiliation route. During a visit with the family doctor, the mother accused Charles of abusing her emotionally and physically. The tactic did not work as I was working with the primary care doctor so he knew the family history. Charles was mortified and, on the advice of the physician and with encouragement from me, he put his mother into a care facility soon after that incident.

I worked with Charles for the next several years and encouraged him to work The Self-Esteem Workbook by Schiraldi, to read CPTSD: From Surviving to Thriving by Pete Walker, The Drama of the Gifted Child by Alice Walker, The Disease To Please by Harriet Braiker, and The Object of My Affection Is in My Reflection by Rokelle Lerner. Both Don and his mother tried to say he deserved the treatment he got from both of them. Turning the shame that Don and his mother shoved into his space into anger for the way he was treated and eventually into compassion for himself and for them was vital to his recovery and continued survival. Charles was finally able to find a psychiatrist who understood PTSD and CPTSD and began taking Zoloft for the off-label use in treatment of PTSD. *(https:// www.psychologytoday.com/blog/the-shrink-tank/201201 /new-treatments-combat-ptsd)*

Don was probably oppositional defiance disordered as a child, and as he became an adult was able to manipulate and harm people under the radar. No remorse. No regret. Occasionally, Charles would come into my office in a panic because Don would send Charles veiled threats through the mail, reminding him of what he did to him, but without ever saying anything incriminating.

Charles cut off all toxic family members and moved without telling anyone except his close friends, me, and the utility company. Only then did he begin to feel safe from the threat of his brother. If what Don told Charles is true, he moved into ASPD as an adult and honed his skills as a predator on prostitutes. His mother was probably a borderline with The Witch type sadism traits. His mother did not live long after she was moved into the care facility.

Before she died Charles confronted his mother with everything that had happened and told her he never wanted to see her again. The mother did not accept responsibility for anything and did not apologize. When the mother died, Charles was relieved. Not every death is a boo hoo hoo. Some deaths are like a weight being lifted, especially if the death is of a parent who was an abuser who caused nothing but fear, self-loathing, and guilt. *(https://www.psychologytoday .com/blog/am-i-normal/201110/ attachment-grief-and-complicated-grief)*

Although Charles still struggles with CPTSD and self-esteem, his physical health has improved. With the death of his mother and his moving residences, the fear has lessened for him, But it is still present if someone reminds him of either his mother or brother. He has the coping skills to deal with the anxiety that arises when triggered, and a large portion of his recovery for him is doing the very hard work of rebuilding his self-esteem. By going to therapy, he recognized that he had value as a human being, as a spiritual being, and that he did not deserve to be harmed by anyone. Part of what helped him was, again, a support system. His wife stood by him and protected him when his mother was living with them and supported the move after the mother died. He learned to rely on good friends and to weed out the ones who were not good friends. Saying no was a new and powerful tool for him. Learning that he had a right to draw boundaries helped him grow and to feel safe again.

Anti-social abusers have absolutely no remorse for what they do. They view their targets as less than human or as objects. That is why incest happens. Usually, the perpetrator is anti-social.

In this next case study the abuse was so extreme the client suffered from Dissociative Identity Disorder (DID) due to the CPTSD.

Bobby, age 62, severe trauma, and reported wanting to deal with the abuse he went through as a child.

Me: "Hey Bobby! How are you? What are we working on today?"

Bonnie: (Very child-like voice and absolutely no eye contact) "I want to work on what happened to me."

Me: "Ok. What happened to you?"

Bobby: (Pulling out an art drawing book) "These are my friends. They keep me safe. This is Tiger (it was a drawing of a cartoon tiger); she protects me. This is Mew Mew (it was a cartoon cat crying); she feels my sad. This is Growler (a cartoon cat who had an angry face); he feels my mad...."

He went on to describe about 12 different cartoon animals, some were male, some were female, that he had drawn and how they all handled different emotions for him. We spent the first session introducing the different cats to me. A few sessions later Bobby felt safe enough to start telling me what happened and why he had cartoon cats handling his emotions.

Bobby: "My dad was mean to me."

Me: "What do you mean, mean to you?"

Bobby: "He would say horrible things to me. He would drink and then come into my bedroom at night."

Me: "How old were you?"

Bobby: (Talking to his cat drawings) "How old was I?" (Then responding) "Three. I was three when he started coming into my bedroom."

Me: "When did he stop?"

Bobby: (Again talking to his cat drawings) "When did he stop? Growler says it was when I left home when I was 18."

Me: "When did Growler and Mew Mew and all the others come along?"

Bobby: "They've been here ever since I can remember. When he would touch me, it was like I was watching it from the ceiling, and then I heard Tiger say she would protect me."

Me: "They did a good job. You are still here!"

Bobby: "I've tried to kill myself. I've cut myself a lot. That is why I wear pants in the middle of the summer, and long sleeves. Tiger doesn't like it when I do that. Usually Growler is the one egging me on. He gets so mad at my dad."

Me: "Understandable."

Bobby: "Dad would lie to Mom. Threaten me. He said he would kill me if I ever told." (He began speaking like a little girl) "You don't think he'll ever know that I told you, do you?"

Me: "No, sweetheart. He will never know."

I worked with him for about six months. This case was absolutely heartbreaking. If it sounds like Sybil, you would not be wrong. Bobby's dad was constantly in and out of jail and prison; he could not hold a job. The mother was an enabler and knew that her husband was molesting their child, but refused to protect Bobby or do anything about it. Bobby's CPTSD was so severe that he literally split off aspects of himself to deal with the abuse. His father was a drug addict, alcoholic, liked to beat the mother and Bobby, and he saw nothing wrong with having sex with his own child. The dad was anti-social, had no remorse, and was sadistic to boot. When Bobby would go home to visit after leaving the house, the father would get him alone and then fondle him and state that he wanted sex from him, demanding he show him his "loyalty" to him by giving into his sexual demands. Bobby felt obligated to visit because of the Fear, Obligation, and Guilt. He also wanted to see his mother.

We worked on self-esteem. We worked on trying to integrate the different aspects of himself. Getting him to see himself as human was a challenge due to the constant betrayal and denial and abuse that his psychopathic father put him through. He ended up moving to New York. I referred him to a specialist in Disassociative Identity Disorder there.

Charles was able to hold himself together, but took the stress of the abuse out on his stomach. Bobby literally split himself into different characters so they could deal with the stress of being abused by a family member with ASPD.

By illustrating the abusers, anti-social, malignant narcissists, and malignant borderlines, you start to get a feel for how abusers abuse and how targets of abuse suffer. So how do predators like the ones I've described choose their targets? Read on to the next chapter to find out!

"Never be bullied into silence.
Never allow yourself to be made a victim.
Accept no one's definition of your life;
define yourself."

Harvey Fierstein

5

THE TARGETS

Why do I like to use the term "target" instead of victim? Victim implies helplessness whereas targets of abuse can and do help themselves if they are done being abused. I also like the term target because predatory abusers pick their target as surely as a hunting Bengal Tiger picks theirs. Make no mistake, abusers seek out people they can easily prey on; they hunt. People are targeted for abuse by predators and are tested and groomed before a relationship ever begins, and the target never even notices it until the abuse begins. *(http://outofthefog.website/top-100-trait-blog/2015/11/4/grooming)*

Targets for abuse usually come from a family of origin in which they were the caregiver in some way, shape, or form. The parents were alcoholic or disabled, and the child had to grow up and take over responsibilities—both physically and emotionally—for the parent. Or the parent was mentally ill or absent so the child had to fend for themselves. Or the target came from a family in which there was abuse, the parents were abusers themselves, or the parents allowed the child to be abused by others. The toxic parents in that case have modeled for the target how relationships look like and, in those instances, relationships are filled with screaming and drama. *(http://www.mdjunction.com/forums/ positive-thinking-discussions/general-support /3000730-inside-the-mind-of-an-abuser-what-you-need-to-kno)* There is a caveat with that: Sometimes the targets of abuse are just kind-hearted, inexperienced, and want to help and/or fix all the ills of the world—which leads me to talk about empaths.

What is an empath? It is a word that gets thrown around…a lot! Empath means the person feels and absorbs the emotions of other people. How many times have you been in a room of people and you knew without anyone saying a word that an argument had happened? Or that someone was sad? Or someone was nervous? Empaths read and take on other people's emotions. If someone is angry, they suddenly become angry. If someone is sad, they become sad. In other words, predators such as malignant narcissists and malignant borderlines have just hit the mother lode of supply. Joy of joys! Someone who they can have absorb all of their nastiness and think that it is theirs! And not only that, but once the malignant person is enraged and the empath starts taking on the anger and mirroring it back, the malignant person can then stop cold, point the finger, and say that it is all the empath's fault: Look how angry and mean they are being to me! *(https://www.psychologytoday.com/blog/ emotional-freedom/ 201602/10-traits-empathic-people-share)*

Malignant narcissists and malignant borderline abusers LOVE to have empaths as partners. Because they, as the predator, do not have emotions, or at least not normal ones, they will berate and put down the empathic partner that does have normal emotions with insults like "You are so sensitive! I was just kidding!" Remember this next line well: Things said in jest are very often meant. Abusers love to use passive aggressive language and will often say what they really think and hide it as "just kidding."

Let's talk about the different traits that abusers go for in a target.

"We Are Lovable. Even if the most important person in your world rejects you, you are still real, and you are still okay."

Melody Beattie,
Codependent No More

6

CODEPENDENT/PEOPLE PLEASER TARGETS

Let's start with a Codependent target first.

Again, all names and identifying characteristics have been changed in these case studies.

Jeremy is 32 years old and a musician. Attractive and athletic. Two boys, ages 10 and 8, from a previous relationship.

Sally also age 32, bookish-looking, and very uptight. She has a son, age 6, from a previous marriage and a son (infant) from this marriage.

Not being able to find a sitter, they brought their newborn son with them to the session.

Me: "So tell me a little bit about you two."

Sally: (Looking at Jeremy)

Jeremy: (Looking uncomfortable)

Me: (Encouraging them to talk) "I understand you have kids." (I say, smiling down at the baby in the carrier.)

Jeremy: (Smiling) "Yeah, I have two boys from my previous relationship, Devon and Harry, 10 and 8, and Sally has Garth who is…?"

Sally: (Rolling her eyes) "Six! He is six, Jeremy! You

should know that!" (Now crossing her arms)

Jeremy: (Attempting to appease Sally) "I'm sorry, babe. I'm a little nervous." (Turning back to the conversation) "So Garth is 6, and we have Gabriel together."

Me: "And how long have you guys been together?"

Sally: "10 months. We started dating, and within a month I got pregnant."

Jeremy: "I used protection."

Sally: (Laughing but a little too hysterically) "I'm just a Fertile Myrtle, I guess!"

Jeremy: "We got married six months ago. It was the right thing to do."

Me: "So, only dated for a month, got pregnant, and now married. Wow."

Sally: "This is exactly what happened in my first marriage."

Me: "You started dating and got pregnant within the first month?"

Sally: "Pretty much. Except that Gerald, my ex, at first didn't want to do the honorable thing, but he did. Then once we were married I was left to take care of the baby by myself. We split last year."

Jeremy: "I do most of the child care. I just want to make Sally's life good."

Me: "So what do you two want to work on?"

Jeremy: "I just, I just can't make her happy! It is my job to make her happy! She has so much fear and insecurity.

I just want to fix all the bad in her life. I want to show her that I'm not Gerald."

Sally: (Nodding her head in agreement)

Me: "Um, guys, we are only responsible for our own happiness, it isn't our job to 'fix' each other. Tell me a little bit about your families, your mom, your dad, caregivers."

Sally: "My dad was an alcoholic, and he split when I was five. My mom was all about her. To this day everything is all about her. Her wants. Her needs. Her emotions."

Me: (Recognizing that she was raised by someone with a personality disorder and an addiction) "So your childhood was…"

Sally: "Lonely. She never would listen to me! Gerald didn't listen to me! I have to scream at Jeremy to get him to listen to me!"

Jeremy: "I'm sorry, babe. I think I'm listening to you…"

Sally: "Well, you're not!" (Her voice raising)

Jeremy: "I'll try harder. I promise."

Me: (Getting a very clear picture of what was going on) "Jeremy, tell me about your family and childhood."

Jeremy: "My dad left when I was two. My mom was working three jobs to keep me and my sister going. I basically raised my sister, and then Mom got sick with cancer. I took care of Mom and my sister, and I started working as soon as I could, odd jobs, musical gigs, I took care of Mom until she died when I was 19. My sister lived with me until she graduated from college. I started bartending when I got old enough."

Me: "Wow. How old where you when she got sick?"

Jeremy: "10."

Me: "So you became the caregiver in the family."

Jeremy: "Yes. I needed to bolster my mom when she was having rough days. And my sister, too, I suppose."

Sally: "You pay so much attention to the kids. I don't feel you pay attention to me!"

Jeremy: "I'm sorry, babe! I will try to do better! I just want to make sure the kids feel loved."

Me: "Jeremy, what are your needs in this relationship?"

Jeremy: "I need Sally to tell me what I am doing right."

Sally: (Immediately defensive) "Yes, but you never tell me what I'm doing right!"

Jeremy: (Exasperated) "Yes, I do!"

Me: "I would really like to see you both individually for a while if that's okay."

Jeremy and Sally: "Ok."

Sally had strong traits of narcissism and BPD due to her mother's obvious narcissism and neglect. Sally had low self-esteem and felt the only way she could get someone to love her was to "make" her partner love her so Sally got pregnant almost as soon as she started dating. Gerald and Jeremy were the only serious relationships she had been in as her narcissistic mother insisted she stay at home and "keep her company." Her mother insisted that no one would love her for her and that she would have to trick them into staying. Consciously or subconsciously, when she started dating Gerald she got pregnant within the first two months of dating and forced Gerald to "do the honorable thing." That marriage was a disaster as the tighter she tried to control Gerald and keep him close like her mother had done to her, the more he slipped through her fingers until they finally divorced after five years of constant fighting, in which she constantly had to be worse off than Gerald. Everything was a competition for who had it worst, according to Sally. Less than a year after divorcing Gerald, she began dating Jeremy; again, consciously or subconsciously, she became pregnant within the first month of dating and Jeremy married her, believing he was doing the "honorable" thing. Again, Sally was attempting to control Jeremy just like she tried to control Gerald by telling him he could not do anything right in the relationship and by trying to keep him with her all the time. Every fight turned into a "Yes, but you did this!" Tit for tat does not work in a healthy relationship, and an eye for an eye will leave the whole world blind. Sally would make progress but then stop coming to counseling for months at a time, only to return when things got bad and by which time she had slid back into unhealthy behaviors.

Jeremy, due to his having been the caregiver and adult at such a young age, felt "responsible" for Sally's emotions and well-being, and Sally was only too happy to let him be. Jeremy worked on his codependency issues by reading and working on books such as The Disease to Please by Harriet Braiker. He, too, would come to therapy for a while and then stop for months at a time, sliding back into unhealthy behaviors. He would justify staying in the relationship because he said he was compassionate and understood her abuse as a child and he didn't want to hurt any of the kids by leaving, even though it was toxic and unhealthy.

Neither one was ready to be healthy. Both wanted to be right. and neither was able to let go of and replace unhealthy communication and develop self-esteem skills. Eventually, they divorced, and both stopped coming to therapy altogether. I have heard all sorts of excuses why people either stay or return or seek out a new abuser. Because of the codependency of the target and the victim role the abuser plays, a target will often say they are being kind and compassionate by staying with their abuser, that their suffering was somehow "noble" because it was "for" this other person who clearly did not give two rats' asses about them.

I want to give another example of codependency. This time from the point of view of a child of an abuser. Kids of abusers are hit the hardest with the codependency. Often an abusive parent will use one or more of the kids as their "confidant" and "therapist," effectively making them "responsible" for the adult's well-being emotionally. Again, all identifying names and traits have been changed.

Clara, age 45, attractive brunette recently divorced from her abuser. She is in a support group and doing well. Clara had the final say in medical and therapy decisions, according to the divorce decree.

Kurt, her 21-year-old son, recently went no contact with his abusive dad and is doing well.

Sarah, her 15-year-old daughter, also recently went no contact with her abusive dad and is depressed and suffering from gnawing guilt.

They came in as a family to support and help Sarah.

> **Me:** "Hey guys! Good to see you! So what brings you in today?"

> **Clara:** "Long story short, I divorced by husband this last January. It was not a healthy relationship. The kids witnessed a lot of verbal and physical fights."

> **Kurt:** "Mom and I decided to go no contact because Dad started trying to get to Mom through me and Sarah. You

know, "Tell your mom this, tell your mom that"—even though they have been divorced for six months and there is nothing that needs to be relayed."

Sarah: (Looking miserable) "I didn't want to go no contact, but I also don't want to go over there and see him. He always tells me bad things about Mom, calls her names, tells me about his love life. It's just, I hate it! I feel like I'm stuck in the middle. If I don't go, he blows my phone up with texts and phone calls berating me for wanting to hang out with my friends! Then he tells me I'm just like Mom."

Me: (Recognizing that the dad was attempting to use the kids as flying monkeys) "So Dad was trying to relay messages, and Kurt and Mom went no contact, and (Looking at Kurt and Clara) you both look happy but Sarah, you look very unhappy."

Sarah: "I am! I don't want to hear what he thinks of Mom! I don't want to know about his love life! I don't want to be over there! But if I don't, he guilts me and tells me I am the reason he is so lonely!"

Clara: "Honey, it isn't your job to take care of him or make him not be lonely."

Sarah: "I just feel so responsible!"

Me: "How was it when he was living at home?"

Sarah and Kurt: "It was awful!"

Kurt: "He would drink and then accuse Mom of everything under the sun. When she tried to leave the room or change the topic, he would become belligerent and start calling her a whore, and when that didn't get the reaction he was looking for he would pin her against the wall and scream in her face. The last fight he started choking her, and I pulled him off of her. Sarah saw all of this."

Sarah: "After every fight he would come find me and tell me how sorry he was and that I shouldn't have to see any of that and that it would never happen again. But then he would cry and tell me that I am the only family member he could talk to."

Me: "Sarah, how long had that been going on?"

Sarah: "Since (Looking at Kurt) I don't know, the last two to three years."

Kurt: (Nodding) "Yeah, at least three years."

Me: "So since you were 12."

Sarah: "Yeah. Kurt is so lucky. He's an adult and isn't forced to go visit."

Me: (Sighing) "Okay. Here is the million-dollar question: If you were not related to him, would you have anything to do with him?"

Kurt and Sarah simultaneously: "NO!"

Me: "Then act accordingly. You are under no obligation to see someone who is causing you suffering."

Clara: "What about the divorce decree?"

Me: "You need to contact your lawyer and set up a meeting with the judge. You can have my records subpoenaed. I can only testify to what is in the medical records, but I am going to recommend that Sarah be allowed to decide for herself whether she wants to continue contact with him."

Sarah: "But he makes me feel so guilty if I don't listen to him! He makes me feel guilty for wanting to hang out with my friends. He makes me feel so guilty for not agreeing with him about Mom!" (Sarah burst into tears.)

Me: "Hon, you just told me that if you were not related to him you would have nothing to do with him. Here is a little secret of the universe: No one, not Dad, not Mom, not me, can MAKE you feel anything. It is a choice, and you can choose to not get hooked by his guilt."

Sarah: "Yes! I don't want anything to do with him, but what if he kills himself?"

Me: "Has he threatened to do that?"

Sarah, Kurt, and Clara: "All the time!"

Clara: "Especially when he thinks he isn't going to get his way."

Me: "You are not responsible for him or his emotions or his actions in any way, shape, or form. He is the adult. If he threatens suicide you are to tell your Mom, and (Looking at Clara) Clara, you are to call the police and have them do a welfare check. You do that each and every time he threatens self-harm. Eventually, he will stop when he realizes that he isn't getting the reaction he is looking for from you."

Sarah: "But what if he does kill himself?"

Me: "It will be his choice and his choice alone."

Sarah: "So how do I deal with him?"

Me: "The best option would be to go no contact. The second best would be to practice something called Grey Rock."

Sarah: "What is that?"

Me: "You stay in touch with him but draw strong boundaries and do not give him any sort of emotional response. Not anger. Not sadness. Not defending your mom. Nothing. Kind of like being a Zen master from a Kung Fu movie."

Kurt: (Turning to Sarah) "So like how I used to do when he was living at home and he tried to start an argument with me. He would poke and poke and poke, and I just refused to give him what he wanted and left the house as soon as I could."

Me: "Exactly. No matter what he says, no matter what he does, you don't give him the emotional response he is looking for."

Sarah: "Sometimes I think he likes to see me in tears."

The family continued to see me for the next year. The dad continued to blow up phones, text, email, and use different phone numbers when they went no contact in an effort to "fool" them into answering the phone. He would also threaten suicide, that is, until Sarah began telling her mom about the suicide threats and Clara began demanding welfare checks and calling the crisis line. The dad tried to say that Clara was harassing him and tried to file a restraining order against her until she showed the judge the texts he had been sending his daughter threatening to kill himself.

Kurt, and eventually Sarah, went no contact and were much, much happier. Eventually, the dad found a new supply with her own kids and stopped contacting Kurt, Sarah, and Clara except for when he married the new woman as he wanted to make sure that they all knew how much happier HE was without them.

Kids are particularly susceptible to the machinations of an abuser because kids naturally think that everything has to do with them. It is a part of the growing process and normal. (http://www.ahaparenting.com/ask-the-doctor-1/is-my-teen-narcissistic-or-just-a-normal-self-centered-teenager) What isn't normal is when a toxic parent starts making others believe that the toxic parent's particular world view is accurate and that the child is responsible for the well-being, emotionally and physically, of the adult abuser. I have had people argue with me on calling crisis or doing welfare checks, saying that "What if the abuser really is suicidal, but now won't say it for fear of having someone show up at their door?" My answer to that is, anytime, ANYTIME, a suicidal threat is made—and especially if it is directed at a child to induce guilt—a crisis team needs to be called. If that person making the suicidal gestures then feels "afraid" to say something about being suicidal, that is THEIR choice. In instances in which the abuser is threatening to a child, I can pretty much guarantee they are not truly suicidal but attempting to control through guilt. I have yet to see an abuser commit suicide when called on the manipulative behavior. Keep in mind I've been doing this since 2005. *(http:// flyingmonkeysdenied.com/2015/12/09/what-is-life-really-like-for-children-of-toxic-or-abusive-parents/)*

"In situations of captivity the perpetrator
becomes the most powerful person in the life of the victim,
and the psychology of the victim is shaped by the actions and
beliefs of the perpetrator."

**Judith Lewis Herman,
Trauma and Recovery: The Aftermath of
Violence – From Domestic Abuse
to Political Terror**

TRAUMA BONDING AND STOCKHOLM SYNDROME TARGETS

"HOW???" you ask. "How do abusers get their targets to not only stay with them, but defend them?? HOW???" One of the things that frustrates loving family members and friends is how in the world someone they love could be abused but then turn around and defend their own abuse. Two phenomena: trauma bonding and Stockholm syndrome.

Trauma bonding by definition is this: It occurs as the result of ongoing cycles of abuse in which the intermittent reinforcement of alternating reward and punishment creates powerful emotional bonds that are very resistant to change. *(https:// en.wikipedia.org/wiki /Traumatic_bonding)*

Stockholm syndrome is a condition that causes hostages to develop a psychological alliance with their captors as a survival strategy during captivity. These feelings, resulting from a bond formed between captor and captives during intimate time spent together, are generally considered irrational in light of the danger or risk endured by the victims. Generally speaking, Stockholm syndrome consists of "strong emotional ties that develop between two persons where one person intermittently harasses, beats, threatens, abuses, or intimidates the other." The FBI's Hostage Barricade Database System shows that roughly 8% of victims show evidence of Stockholm syndrome. *(https:// en.wikipedia.org/wiki/Stockholm_syndrome* and *http://www. encyclopedia.com/social-sciences/applied-and-social-sciences-*

magazines /traumatic-bonding)

Also, if the abuser is a romantic partner, they are bonding sexually with the target of abuse. Oxytocin is a powerful bonding hormone that is produced from skin to skin contact. It is the hormone that helps bond babies and mothers. Unfortunately, it is also what helps bond targets to abusers. Abusers will often use sex—especially in the love bombing phase—to entrap their target and bond them to them. Remember: Love bombing is the manipulative technique that abusers use of showering the target with affection and constant contact with them in the beginning of the relationship, in order to draw the target in and ensnare them. This is different from healthy affection and attention in the beginning of a relationship in that healthy attention is never in the extreme. Love bombing creates limerence. Limerence is the state of being infatuated or obsessed with another person, typically experienced involuntarily and characterized by the strong desire for reciprocation. It usually lasts from 18 months to three years. *(https://www.psychologytoday.com/blog/here-there-and-everywhere/201209/limerence-in-love-obsessed-or-both)* One of the reasons it is so hard to break an abuser's grip is, well, the damn hormone oxytocin. If the target is having regular physical (read sex) contact with the abuser, there is a chemical bond happening that makes the target much less interested in leaving the bond. *(Getting Close by Lisa A. Philips, Psychology Today, February 2017, 50 –51)* The abuser will use sex as a weapon, lavishing sex upon the target at first and establishing the bond, but then will, over time, cut the sex down or off altogether.

Interestingly, when an abuser begins to pull away, the target of abuse will release a huge amount of oxytocin in an effort to reestablish contact with the abuser. So the intermittent positive rewards not only release serotonin, dopamine, and endorphins but oxytocin, which tells the brain that you must stay with this person. It is truly a case of the target being addicted to the abuser. *(https://www.psychologytoday.com/blog/science-choice/201411/addiction-disease-isolation; see also https://www.*

psychologytoday.com/blog/the-athletes-way/ 201705/face-face-connectedness-oxytocin-and-your-vagus-nerve)

The following is a case study illustrating both Stockholm syndrome and trauma bonding. All identifying names and characteristics have been changed.

I received a frantic call from a mom. She was convinced her adult daughter Joann was in danger. The daughter was dating and living with a man who was older than her and, in their opinion, very controlling to the point in which she was limited in her contact with both her family and her old friends. The daughter could not come to the counseling session, but the mom, dad, and brother could.

Jane Hudson, the mom, 56 years old, very athletic and young-looking.

David Hudson, the dad, also 56 years old; also very athletic and young-looking.

Brian Hudson, the older brother, 26 years old and also very athletic.

> **Me:** "Hi! Come on in. So I understand there is a family member you are concerned about."

> **Jane:** "Brian found your videos on YouTube. You are describing what our daughter, Joann, is going through."

> **Me:** "How old is Joann?"

> **David and Jane together:** "21."

> **Jane:** "She just turned 21 last week."

> **Me:** "Okay, so she is an adult. So what is going on?"

Brian: "She started dating this creep, Ted, about a year ago, and he is doing to her everything you described in your videos about abusers."

[For those who do not know, I post to YouTube my Facebook mental health talk show *We Need To Talk, with Kris Godinez.* Prior to getting the show going, I posted videos on various mental health and social issues.]

David: "We just don't know what to do! She is not doing well; he has cut her off from her family and friends and convinced her that every good thing we have ever done or are doing for her is bad!"

Jane: "He tells her that staying in touch with us is unhealthy for her."

Brian: "Her friends are calling me, wanting to know what the heck is going on, why she won't hang out with them anymore."

Me: "Ok. Start at the beginning. Give me a broader picture of what is going on."

David: "She WAS going to college to get her degree in art."

Jane: "She met this 30-year-old at one of her art exhibits, and he swept her off her feet."

David: "She called me up and told me he was Mr. Wonderful, so kind and caring, and really got her. She said that he swept her off her feet, like a fairytale prince."

Brian: "At first she would bring him over to my house and to Mom and Dad's house. But, man, my skin just crawled every time he came over."

Jane and David: "Us, too!"

Me: "How so? Tell me more."

Brian and Jane and David all kind of looked at each other. David indicated that Brian should go first.

Brian: "He was trying too hard. I don't know how to explain it, but he wanted to be buddy-buddy with me. When I talked about what I do for a living, which is computers, suddenly he started lecturing ME about computers, like he knew all about programming."

Me: "What does he do for a living?"

Brian: "He works at a freaking call center doing collections. He doesn't even have a college degree. He says he dropped out so he could have 'real-life experiences' like he couldn't learn real life at college."

Me: "Ah."

Jane: "Brian is absolutely right. He was just trying too hard. He would call us (indicating her and David) 'Mom' and 'Dad' the first time he met us, and that just rubbed both of us the wrong way."

Brian: "I met him at a coffee shop with Joann, and right after he sent me a friend request on both my Instagram and my Facebook profile. I didn't accept because I didn't know who he was in the real world, and my first impression of him was not good. I asked him to go out to coffee or lunch with me several times but he always had an excuse as to why he couldn't meet. Sarah, my sister's best friend, told me he friended her immediately after meeting her, too; she accepted the friend request but, here is the weird thing, he never engaged with Sarah, never liked anything. Sarah felt like he just wanted to be able to lurk and figure her out."

Jane: "Joann invited him to dinner to meet us. We aren't super religious, but he started talking about how atheists are better than religious people and how he is an atheist. Then he asked David what he thought."

David: "I said we are not religious but that we do believe in God."

Jane: "His whole demeanor changed. He stuttered something like 'Uh, er, well, really I'm more agnostic than atheist.' And then quickly changed the subject."

David: "Joann used to be the most joyous person you would ever meet. Fun. Filled with joy. Always joking, but when she brought Ted around she stopped, and if she did try to make a joke, Ted would put her down and basically tell her that her humor was immature."

Me: (Raising my eyebrows) "Really?"

Brian: "It's like he was jealous of her getting any attention at all."

Jane: "The thing that scared me was that Joann started spending every waking moment with him; every free weekend she had he was there. There was never a time when any of us could be alone with Joann."

David: "I told Joann my concerns as her grades started slipping, and she actually yelled at me, telling me it was her life and she was an adult and she knew what she was doing."

Jane: "Ted would subtly put her down. She stopped being her, and she became someone none of us recognize."

Brian: "I tried talking to her as well. She ran back to Ted and told him every concern I had. It wasn't long before Ted sent me an email demanding that I apologize to him for what I said to Joann in confidence. I never did apologize, and I won't—especially because I never said my concerns to him, I told Joann."

David: "It became clear she was going back and telling Ted any and everything we said about our concerns. He didn't dare pull the email thing with Jane and me, but what he did do is start telling Joann that he didn't want her around her family anymore as we were a 'bad influence' on her."

Jane: "It wasn't long before Ted told her to stop seeing her friends. Her best friend, Sarah, the one she had since she was a teenager, told her she was seeing red flags, and Joann ran back to Ted and told him what Sarah said."

Brian: "Sarah came to me and told me that Joann stopped returning her calls and started getting very nasty with her when they did talk. Ted only wants her to hang out with his friends, but she told me that he accuses her of flirting with them when she does. And I've met Ted's friends; it is like they are all mini versions of Ted. Not only that but Ted unfriended Sarah soon after she told Joann her concerns, and apparently Ted told Joann to stop talking to Sarah."

Jane: "We all saw her changing. The worst was when she began lying."

David: "She tried telling Brian that 'Everybody lies.'"

Brian: (Nodding.) "It was unbelievable. Joann was always honest and always valued the truth. Suddenly, we all started catching her in lies, and it sounded like it was words coming straight out of Ted's mouth. It wasn't the way she would think, let alone talk."

David: "We asked Joann to go to counseling and at first she did, until she started recognizing that Ted was abusive."

Jane: "Suddenly, she stopped going. We got a nasty screaming phone call from Ted, demanding that we apologize and tell Joann that he was perfect for her, that we were horrible parents, that he was going to make sure that Joann never would be with us again, that he didn't want her talking to Brian or going on family vacations. He wanted her to drop out of college. He accused Brian of having incestuous thoughts about Joann! Just all sorts of crazy things!"

David: "I told him he wasn't welcome in our home or our family"

Brian: (Muttering under his breath) "Sick son of a bitch!"

Jane: "We haven't heard from her in three months. She has gone out for coffee with Brian every once in a while, but we suspect Ted doesn't know that she's talking to Brian."

Brian: "Yeah, but we never talk about Ted. I don't dare. I'm the only one she's having contact with, and I'm pretty sure she isn't telling Ted we go out for coffee. It's just weird talking to her, one minute she will be my little sis and the next minute she is rewriting history and putting words into Mom and Dad's mouth that I KNOW were never said."

Me: "Ok, well, I can't diagnose or work on either Joann or Ted since they are not sitting in front of me. I can recommend that you read a couple of books that may help you. One is The Object of My Affection Is in My Reflection: Coping With a Narcissist by Rokelle Lerner. The other is The Disease To Please by Harriet Braiker."

Brian: "That second book is Joann, totally. She is a total people pleaser."

Jane: "That first book is Ted, we think, because he plays the victim all the time and is a know-it- all. We think that he's a Covert narcissist. That and all the videos you've done on abuse describe what is happening to our daughter."

Me: "Ok. Good. You've done your homework!"

David: "How do we help her? How do we help her see how she has changed? She keeps telling Brian that we just don't understand and that we should be more accepting and compassionate."

Me: "Wow. Here is the deal: The more you push, the more of a Romeo/Juliet scenario you create. It's known as the 'backfire effect.' The more you try to convince Joann she is wrong and that you are right, the more she will cling tenaciously to her mistaken belief. (https://youarenotsosmart.com/2011/06/10/the-backfire-effect/) You all tried to tell her of your concerns but she A. Didn't want to hear them and B. Ran back to the person you are concerned about, who it sounds like he twisted it and made you guys the 'problem' in their relationship."

Jane: "Oh absolutely. In that phone call when Ted was screaming at us, he said we were the reason that he and Joann were having problems, and they had been only dating for less than a year at that point."

Brian: "Yeah. I just had coffee with her last week and she was telling me how much better she and Ted are getting along now that she isn't 'influenced' by Mom and Dad. I'm calling bullshit! (Looking over at Jane and David) Pardon my mouth. Just two weeks ago she was terrified because they had had yet another screaming argument and he threatened to leave her."

Jane: (Reaching over and patting his knee) "No, honey, we all agree it is bullshit."

David: "So how do we help her?"

Me: "Ah. Therein lies the sticky wicket. She has become

completely emotionally dependent on this guy; he sounds like he needs a third party to create an 'us vs. them' situation so he can be the victim. That is known as triangulation, wherein the abuser has a third person or party to use as the villain so the target is focused on who the abuser says is the villain instead of the real villain, which is the abuser."

David: "Brian said Ted told her to drop out of school and just sell her art, and that he would take care of her financially."

Me: "Wow. Has she?"

Jane and David: "We don't know. She isn't talking to us."

Brian: "As far as I know, no, not yet. But he keeps telling her how much money she is going to make selling her art. Kris, there is a reason artists are known as 'starving artists.'"

Me: "Yeah, I know. So it sounds like he wants her isolated and to be completely emotionally AND financially dependent on him."

David: "Exactly. How do we get her away from him?"

Me: "You don't. All you can do is be there for her, continue to be consistent, call her on her lies, correct the gaslighting that Ted tries to perpetuate. Brian, keep up that contact so she has some grounding to the real world."

Jane: (Desperate) "But, but, you know about this kind of abuse. There must be something we can do!"

Me: "Like I said, I don't have them in front of me. However, based on the behavior, what it sounds like is going on is gaslighting, which is rewriting history, trauma bonding, and Stockholm syndrome. He's lying to her, villainizing the very family and friends who love her, in order to isolate her. They are obviously having arguments. So my guess is that there is trauma bonding going on. In other words, he runs hot and cold, keeping her on her toes, which is known as trauma bonding using intermittent positive rewards. It is just like when you train an animal to behave in a certain way, you don't always give a "treat." The treat in the abuser's world is to behave nice. You abuse, abuse, abuse, and then behave nice and again behave nice for a while, and then scream at the target of abuse so that the target begins to live for the times when the abuser is kind to them. Couple this with making the target of abuse dependent on the abuser for emotional comfort, given that the abuser has now isolated the target of abuse from friends and family and is attempting to make the target abuse financially dependent as well. The target's well-being, both emotionally and physically, now depends on the abuser, thereby setting up the Stockholm syndrome in which an abused target's brain is so brainwashed by the gaslighting and dependency that they will irrationally turn their back on the family and friends who truly love and care about them and defend the very person who is the one lying to them and abusing them. It was named after a situation in Stockholm, Sweden, in which hostages after only a week of intermittent positive rewards were attempting to protect their hostage takers when the police finally got in to free them."

David: "Holy shit."

Jane: (In tears) "So there's nothing we can do? Nothing?"

Me: "She is an adult. Legally, all you can do is very carefully call out the behavior, have good boundaries, don't put up with her trying to gaslight you, and be prepared for flying monkeys if and when she does leave him. Educate the living crap out of yourself on abuse so you recognize his behavior and hers. Remind her of who she was before she got together with Ted. You are going to have to repeat that she deserves better often and replace the narrative with a positive one. You don't want the backfire effect." (see Adam Ruins Everything TV series, Season 2, Episode 8: "Emily Ruins Adam")

Jane: "Flying monkeys?"

Me: "His family or friends or, as I like to call them, minions doing abuse by proxy, trying to get her to come back to him should she ever successfully leave."

There was silence for a while.

Brian: "Have we lost her forever?"

Me: "I'm not a fortune teller. Some people leave the abuse, others stay, and still others leave only to return to the original abuser or they find a new abuser. It depends on whether or not they ever work on themselves and recognize that neither they, nor their family nor friends, deserve to be treated poorly. It hinges on whether or not they are done being abused."

Joann was young and very empathic. Her abuser was almost nine years older than her. She is one of the exceptions that I mentioned earlier; she came from a relatively normal, supportive family. *(https://www.elephantjournal.com/2017/06/from-genetics-to-trauma-4-reasons-why-people-become-empaths/)*

Once the family removed itself from the equation and stopped being adamant about Ted, but still maintained healthy boundaries, Ted grew bored and looked hard to find another triangulation so that Joann wouldn't figure it out that Ted was, in fact, the problem. At first, he tried to triangulate with the brother, Brian, but Brian steadfastly refused to talk about Ted to Joann so he could maintain contact. Brian was smart to not discuss Ted with Joann because Joann did not feel compelled to run back to Ted and tell him anything. Ted wasn't getting the drama he wanted, and torturing Joann was not as fun without a villain in the picture. He demanded she quit school and not work and do her art, and she did. But when she failed to sell, like he kept insisting she could, he then berated her and put her down, and then the devalue and discard phase began in earnest.

Joann eventually left, two years after she quit school. On average, it takes an abuse victim anywhere between two and five years to leave an abusive relationship and something like seven attempts of trying to leave before they are able to do so. *(http:// www .domesticabuseshelter.org/infodomesticviolence.htm)*

So what was the event that finally allowed Joann to leave? Ted was in a fit of rage because she wasn't selling her art fast enough for him. He picked up her art supplies and threw them at her, one by one, missing her by inches. He then raged at her for hours, spitting in her face as he screamed at her, calling her names like 'incompetent,' 'immature,' 'idiot,' 'stupid,' and worse.

Joann was lucky in that she had the connection through Brian to reconnect with a loving support system and leave. She later told me that she thought she was being 'noble' and 'honorable' to stay with him and stand up for him since no one in the family liked him. She had the mistaken belief that she had to excuse and defend him from the reality that her family and friends were trying to point out. *(http://flyingmonkeysdenied.com/2016/05/23/ how-to-stop-feeling-sorry-for-narcopaths-and-other-toxic-people/)* She suffered a great deal of cognitive dissonance and could not remember entire episodes that happened, especially when the reality of the abuse clashed with the constant gaslighting lies the abuser, Ted, fed her on a daily basis. *(https:// www.elephantjournal.com/2016/10/living-with-c-ptsd-following-an-abusive-relationship/)*

One of the hardest things for Joann to deal with was when Ted attempted to "Hoover" her back.

Me: "Hey Joann! How are you doing today?"

Joann: (Tearful) "I miss him so badly! I just keep thinking about all the good times we had!"

Me: (Recognizing the abuse amnesia and the possible interference by Ted the abuser in his Hoovering) "Ok. What's going on? Last week you were telling me how he put you down and forced you into choosing between your family and him."

Joann: "He has been texting me nonstop. He called me."

Me: (Now worried, knowing that Hoovering especially right after leaving is very dangerous for the target of abuse) "I thought you blocked him."

Joann: "I did. He has been texting and calling me from his friend's phone or from numbers I don't recognize."

Me: "Sweetie, you need to block ALL numbers he tries to contact you from. These are not people you want to have contact with anyway. They are being his flying monkeys."

Joann: "I know! I know! But it's like, it's like I want so desperately to have him back. I mean, (Looking very confused) Not, the him who was throwing things at me and screaming at me, but that sweet guy, the one who swept me off my feet!"

Me: "Honey, that guy never truly existed. That was what is known as love bombing. What you wish for is to reunite with the mask he wore when he was love bombing you."

Joann: "Yes! I want that him back. That him must be in there somewhere!"

Me: "Joann, you cannot fix him because you did not break him."

Joann: (Wailing) "But I want to! I want my Ted back!"

Me: "Tell me what was said in the texts and phone calls."

Joann: "Basically, that he was sorry and he didn't mean any of it and that he wants me back and I am the only one who can save him from himself."

Me: (Trying very hard not to roll my eyes) "Joann, he is Hoovering you to get you back into his life. Just like the vacuum cleaner, he is trying to suck you back into his vortex of abuse. Actions always speak louder than words. Is he in therapy?"

Joann: "No."

Me: "Is he working on himself in any way?"

Joann: "No."

Me: "Is he still subtly making you responsible for his well-being?"

Joann: (Thinking a minute and clearly debating with herself) "Yes."

Me: "The only person who can save him from himself is, well, him, not you."

Joann: "It's like he almost knows when I'm doing well, and then he starts trying to find a way to have an excuse for me to talk to him. I do miss how he was in the beginning."

Me: "How he was in the beginning was an illusion. It was one of the many masks he wears to draw people in. People who truly love you do not isolate you from supportive friends and family. People who truly love you do not sabotage you and set you up for failure, like Ted did by isolating you from your mom and dad and by forcing you to drop out of school and then berate you for not selling enough of your art work. True love is supportive and kind, never cruel or snarky or mean."

Joann: "He was so sarcastic. Always complaining about everything not being good enough."

Me: "True love finds the silver lining in almost every situation."

Joann: "That wasn't love, was it?"

Me: "I think for you, it was love. I know you did love him, but I do not believe for one hot second that he truly loved or loves you. Abusers do not understand love. I think in the beginning for you it was infatuation because of how he love bombed you. For him, you are nothing more than a supply for his ego to feed off of."

Joann: "I've been reading the books you suggested, and that's what they said in there, too."

Me: "That's why I wanted you to read those books so you know that it's not an opinion and I'm not just talking out of my ass." (She smiled, and I said, after a pause) "Block all the numbers. Don't even read the texts. I want you to write a goodbye letter to him NOT to be sent. In it I want you to write down the good, the bad, the ugly, the horrific and, at the end, punt him out of your head. Tell him you are raising the rent and you no longer want him in your life or in your head. Trot it out to the barbecue, read it out loud once, then burn it. You may want to jot down the horrible things he did to you and keep it handy to remind yourself of the abuse you went through physically and emotionally so when he tries to Hoover you, you have a reminder of why you left."

Joann: "Ok. (She looked sad and scared.) Writing the letter is going to be hard. (Then she thought of her future, which was a good sign.) "How do I stay out of another abusive relationship? How will I not make the same mistakes?"

Me: "You have got to learn self-esteem, boundaries, and have a deal breaker list. If that person does anything on the deal breaker list that will include isolating or attempting to isolate you from supportive family and friends, you drop them like a hot potato!"

Joann was as addicted to Ted as an addict is to a substance. Through the trauma bonding, drama, and Stockholm syndrome, I had to treat her as if I was dealing with someone leaving a substance. When I deal with someone getting sober from a substance, I have them write a goodbye letter to their drug of choice. This is what I had Joann do with Ted. In her goodbye to him, she mourned the loss of the guy she first met, the one who swept her off of her feet; she mourned the loss of the mask he wore to seduce her through the love bombing phase. Then she went through when the mask started to slip, how he started to isolate her and rage at her and in the end threatened her physically. At the end of her letter she told him goodbye in no uncertain terms, raised the rent, and evicted him.

When my substance addicts write a letter, their drug of choice writes them a letter back. In the letter back, I remind them of what the substance will do to them if they continue taking it, spiritually, mentally, physically, and otherwise. In the letter back from the abuser/substance, I remind the client of what will happen to them if they stay with the abuser, based on how the abuser abused. It is often an eye-opener and puts an end to the magical thinking that somehow they could just "love" their abuser into sanity.

Once Ted realized that Joann had blocked all numbers and wasn't going to play, or buy into the Hoover maneuver, he quickly moved on to another young woman and then tried to taunt Joann with the fact that he had moved on, sending messages through flying monkeys to her, until she finally blocked all flying monkeys.

The Hoover can happen anywhere from right after the breakup to decades later. Narcissistic abusers need an ego supply to feed off of, and they will return to a previous supply if no new fresh supply is available. It is imperative for the target of abuse to get strong, get out of the Fear, Obligation, and Guilt (F.O.G.), and work on their self-esteem and codependency issues so that when, not if but when, the abuser decides to Hoover, the target is no longer an easy mark. *(http://www.goodtherapy.org/blog/hoover-maneuver-the-dirty-secret-of-emotional-abuse-0219154)*

"Family is supposed to be
our safe haven. Very often it is the place
where we find our deepest heartache."

Iyanla Vanzant

TOXIC PARENTS AND GRANDPARENTS

Toxic parents don't stop being toxic when the kids grow up. It drives me crazy when I hear a client say that some outsider or, in a lot of cases, some family flying monkey is making them wrong for having gone Grey Rock or no contact with a toxic parent. Usually, the bullshit that the flying monkey does is try to guilt trip them and usually with the Bible. The most frequent citing is that of Ephesians 6:2: "Honor thy mother and father." However, what the flying monkeys ignore is the very next line, Ephesians 6:4, which says: "Do not provoke your children to anger." Hate to break it to all the religious flying monkeys out there, but respect is a two-way street. Even in the Bible.

Here is an example of a toxic parent tormenting a grown child. Again, all names and identifying characteristics have been changed.

Simon, age 33, and Meagan, also age 33, have two kids, ages 5 and 6. Coming in to work on strengthening their relationship and deal with Meagan's overbearing Mom.

Me: "Hey Guys! So in-law issues?"

Simon: (Rolling his eyes) "You have no idea!"

Meagan: "It's my mother. She has just been awful, and it is affecting our relationship and hurting our kids."

Me: "What's going on?"

Meagan: (Sighing) "It started when we got married. My mom refused to go to our wedding. She said I was betraying her."

Simon: "It was weird because she acted like she liked me, but she was just angry that Meagan was getting married."

Meagan: "On our wedding day she claimed she was sick."

Simon: "I don't think she really was."

Meagan: "Me either."

Me: "How long have you been married?"

Meagan: "12 years."

Simon: "And right after we got married, her attitude toward me changed, and I don't know why."

Meagan: "She has always had money. She and Dad have been divorced for, God, at least 20 years. But it was like she started throwing money at me and encouraged me to go do things with just her and not bring Simon. Then we had our first baby, Ryan, and she lavished gifts on him. But her gifts always came with strings attached. I felt like I had to be at her beck and call."

Simon: "Then we had Jacob, and it got worse. The reason we are here is because she has been bad-mouthing me to Meagan, and I want Meagan to stand up to her."

Me: "What do you mean bad-mouthing?"

Meagan: "She gets drunk and then calls and starts telling me how Simon doesn't make enough money and that I should pack up the kids and move in with her, that she would take care of us."

Simon: "I make damn good money, and I am a damn good husband and father."

Meagan: "You are! The final straw came when we decided we were going to take the kids to Disneyland for the first time. She offered to pay for everything but she wanted to go."

Simon: "So as tactfully as we could we told her that we wanted to do just the four of us and not to worry about paying. Well, that pissed her off. I tried to tell her we could do another vacation with her next year."

Meagan: "So we get to Disneyland. We are staying at the Disney hotel and, not two hours into being there and checking in, she calls me and demands that I fly home to take care of her."

Me: "What?"

Meagan: "Keep in mind this woman has a full-time paid companion."

Me: "What was her reasoning?"

Meagan: "I don't know because she was really drunk when she called. She started calling Simon names and me names, and then she threatened to kill herself because she said I wasn't paying enough attention to her"

Me: "Oh, Good God!"

Simon: "So here we are on what we thought was going to be an awesome family vacation having to deal with my insane mother-in-law."

Me: "So what did you do?"

Meagan: "Simon got on his phone and started calling other family members, explaining the situation. Finally, my cousin Marci was able to go over and stay with her. But then, Marci tells me that Mom got onto Facebook and her phone and started telling the rest of the family how selfish Simon and I are and what horrible people we are."

Me: "Has she always been like this?"

Meagan: "That is pretty much why Dad divorced her. She has always had a problem with alcohol but she has also always raged and said bad things about family members who piss her off."

Simon: "So when we got back from Disney, I told Meagan that was it. Meagan was a wreck the entire time we were there, checking her phone constantly, worried that her mother would make good on her threats to kill herself even though Marci was there with her."

Meagan: "I just feel so guilty! She IS my mother, even though Dad pretty much raised me."

Me: "Okay. Here's the question I ask everyone when they feel obligated to a family member, even when the behavior is outrageous: If you were not related to her, would you have anything to do with her?"

Meagan: (Almost relieved) "No. I wouldn't have anything to do with her."

Me: "Then act accordingly."

Meagan: "But what about the kids? I feel like a bad daughter for taking their grandmother away from them!"

Me: "Does she treat them the same way she treats you? Like they owe her?"

Simon: "Actually, yeah. Ryan told me that he didn't like being over there when she was drinking."

Me: "You are not being a bad daughter, and if the woman is drinking, you don't want the kids over there anyway."

Meagan: (Thinking) "Yeah, even Jake doesn't want to be over there, especially recently."

Me: "Then don't worry about them spending time with her. The way she is behaving is not healthy and not a good role model for them."

Meagan: "So what do I do? How do I disentangle us from her?"

Me: "You have two options: You either limit time around her and learn to not respond to her histrionics, a technique called going Grey Rock, or you go no contact."

I worked with Simon and Meagan over the next six months, teaching them about healthy communication and using the Grey Rock technique in dealing with Meagan's mother. Meagan would stop her mom from putting Simon down, and when the Mom realized that Meagan and Simon had taken control back over their lives, she disowned them and continued to try to use suicidal threats to make Meagan pay attention to her. When none of that worked, she threatened to try to take custody of their children. She never did follow through on that threat, but she made it frequently, which was stressful to Meagan and Simon. Because Simon and Meagan were married, the mom could not follow through with it. But in this next case study, the grandmother did follow through with her threat of dragging the couple into court for custody of the grandkids.

Again, all identifying characteristics and names have been changed.

In lo, these many years I have been working with targets of

abuse, the most frustrating is when an abuser decides to interfere with a grandchild and invokes "grandparents rights." In the State of Arizona grandparents can demand visitation rights if the parent of the child has been divorced for three months or longer, the other parent is deceased three months or longer, or the parents were never married. (http://www.jacksonwhitelaw.com/arizona-family-law/grandparents-visitation-rights/)

Don't get me wrong; in some cases having grandparents rights is a good thing, especially if it is an abuser who is playing an alienation game with the abused divorced spouse so at least the grandparents of the divorced spouse can have an influence on the kids for the better. This isn't one of those cases. This is a case in which you wish the judges had more training in personality disorders.

Paula, age 37, with dark short hair, is attractive and physically fit, and Brent, also age 37, with short blonde hair is also attractive and physically fit; never married, they have one child together, Selah, age six. Separated due to interference from Brent's mother, but now back together and working on the relationship.

Me: "Hey Paula, Brent! What do you want to work on today?"

Paul: "It's his mother…again."

Brent: "She is demanding 'grandparent visiting rights.'"

Me: "What?"

Paula: "We just got a letter from an attorney saying that she filed for visitation rights. This was after Brent went low contact when he figured out that she had been lying to him and interfering with our relationship."

Me: (Looking at Brent) "Ok. Tell me more what happened."

Brent: (Looking at Paula) "I think you tell it better than I do."

Paula: (Shrugging) "So Brent's mom would come and spend the winter with us; she has done this ever since her husband died ten years ago. It would range from anywhere from a couple of months to six months if she was having medical issues."

Brent: (Adding to the conversation) "My mom needed a pacemaker. Heart issues. Fainting."

Paula: (Continuing) "So the visits were always...difficult. Rosalee, his mom, is very demanding, and it got worse when Selah was born."

Brent: "It was weird. It was like she wanted Selah to be hers, and she would get angry if Paula did any of the normal mothering."

Paula: "When I returned to work after having Selah, I would be up early and take Selah to day care because I didn't want Rosalee to have the burden of caring for a newborn, especially since she was having heart issues. But here is where it gets really odd: She started telling Brent that I wasn't doing enough housework, that I wasn't 'contributing' enough, that I wasn't a good mother, and that I didn't pay enough attention to Selah or to her and that she was having to keep the house. She also accused me of spending Brent's hard-earned money. She was jealous because I would take time to work out with our trainer and go to the gym and get my hair and nails done. God forbid if I brought takeout food home. Nothing I did was good enough. I even pointed out to her that I spent my own money on myself for the hair and nails, but that didn't matter."

Brent: "I am sorry to say that I believed what my mother was telling me. I mean, she's my mom, right? She is supposed to have my best interests at heart." (At this point he shook his head.) "She didn't. Paula and I got into some pretty horrific screaming matches while she was living with us, especially that last year."

Paul: "It got to the point at which she was absolutely making things up about me that were completely untrue and easily debunked. Like her accusing me of frivolous spending. She also twisted every good thing I had ever done for Brent into something manipulative and evil, and he started to believe it! That was the mind-blowing thing! The final straw for me was her cornering me sobbing, literally right after Brent left for work, like the door just finished closing and she had me cornered in the kitchen, sobbing and saying that I needed to make her happy and it was my fault she was unhappy because I had taken her baby away from her. It was insane."

Me: "When you say her baby?"

Paula: "She meant both Selah and Brent."

Brent: "Mom lied to me and told me that Paula cornered her and was screaming at her. Because I wanted to believe my mother, I was treating Paula poorly, not listening to her, not believing her, only believing what my mother told me. Paula took Selah and moved out. I should have known that my mother was lying. She would listen to our arguments and just grin like it was exactly what she wanted."

Me: "Holy Mackerel! So how long were you separated? How did you figure it out and get back together?"

Brent: (Smiling and taking Paula's hand) "Thankfully, we were only separated a couple of months. She (Nodding at Paula) didn't give up on me. Paula also audiotaped that conversation on her phone. When Mom went back home for the summer, Paula and I started talking again. I listened to the tape and realized my mom had totally lied to me about everything. At first, I wanted to make Paula wrong for taping it because I wanted to believe my mom. Paula demanded I go see a counselor, and she found your videos and the book recommendations. I watched your videos and read The Object of My Affection Is in My Reflection: Coping With a Narcissist by Rokelle Lerner, and I recognized my mother and her divide and conquer behavior. Plus, my mother was saying things like 'You don't need Paula, you just need me.' It was scary how close I came to losing Paula and Selah."

Me: "So are you seeing an individual counselor then?"

Brent: "Yeah, I'm seeing a counselor in Scottsdale that specializes in helping adult children of personality disordered parents."

Paula: "She recommended you to Brent for couples therapy to work on the issue of his mother, which we both have."

Me: (Nodding.) "Okay. Got it! So you have been going to individual therapy, working on the issues with your mom, you guys got back together…"

Brent: "And now my mother is pissed because I went Grey Rock with her and refused to let her come down for the wintertime anymore."

Paula: "She has filed with the court, demanding grandparent visitation rights. The crazy thing is that she has been leaving messages on our phones, telling us that she is going to take Selah away from us."

Me: "You realize she doesn't have a legal leg to stand on?"

Paula and Brent: "No."

Brent: "She hired this real douchebag of a lawyer, and he has been intimating that we will lose Selah."

Me: "Have you hired a family law attorney yet?"

Paula: "Yes. We are going to meet with him this afternoon. We wanted to get going with the counseling because I know this is going to be stressful."

Me: "Okay, make sure he understands personality disorders. You need to document EVERYTHING. Do you still have the tape?"

Paula: "Yes."

Me: "Okay. Talk to your attorney. Whether it is admissible or not is a question for your attorney. As far as you as a couple are concerned, NOTHING is to be discussed over the phone with her. Make it all emails or texts so you have it in writing."

Brent: "She plays dumb when it comes to technology so she won't text. She might email."

Me: "Then save every single voice mail you get. Force her to do email. How are you guys doing as a couple, and how is Selah?"

Brent: "We are doing much better. We stopped having contact with Mom six months ago. I don't let her talk to Paula on the phone. I had been letting her do Facetime with Selah but she started bad-mouthing Paula to Selah."

Me: "Wait a minute, you just said she played dumb with technology but she does Facetime?"

Paula: "She plays dumb when it works to her advantage."

Me: "Okay, so Brent, you're going to have to monitor any time she spends with Selah. And if and when she starts to bag on Paula, you immediately either end the conversation or correct her so there is no question of what you will and will not put up with."

Brent: "Okay."

Me: "I want you guys to communicate like nobody's business. Abusive parents seek to divide and conquer and will lie to instill doubt in the adult child about their spouse."

Paula: (Laughing) "That won't be a problem. Brent and I are reading and watching everything we can on good communication skills, and we check in with each other daily."

Me: "Good! Okay, so now here is what you need to be prepared for, if she is an abusive narcissist..."

Brent: "She is."

Me: (Nodding and continuing.) "Then you need to be prepared to fight the battle of your lives. She and her douchebag lawyer will try to wear you down and drag things out. That is why you need a family law attorney who gets that he may be dealing with someone with a personality disorder on the opposing side. This isn't going to go away quickly, and you need to steel yourselves that this could take a year or more to resolve."

Brent: (Squeezing Paula's hand) "There's no way in hell I'm going to let her win."

Paula: "As long as Brent keeps himself grounded and clear and continues therapy and we both work on ourselves and us, we got this!"

Long story short, the mom, Rosalee, dragged them through

the court system for three years. Rosalee perjured herself multiple times, would feign not remembering, had her attorney file frivolous motion after frivolous motion, and accused the couple of everything under the sun including incest and child abuse. Child Protection Services (CPS) got involved, and all accusations were found baseless. The initial judge retired and was replaced by a judge who did not cater to abusers and saw through the ploys of Rosalee and her attorney. By the time the new judge took over, Selah was nearing nine years old and told the court-ordered counselor that she did not want to see her grandmother at all. The new judge took that into consideration and finally dismissed the case. It didn't hurt that Brent and Paula decided to marry since in Arizona grandparent rights carry more weight if the couple is not married.

The toll it took on Paula and Brent and Selah was huge. During the court case Selah was forced to do supervised visits with the grandmother who would try to guilt trip her, bribe her, and gaslight her. Both Paula and Brent almost had a nervous breakdown due to the stress. They had to spend thousands of dollars to keep Brent's mother out of their lives, even though they were a couple raising their child together. But because in Arizona they were not married, the grandmother had the right to petition for visitation, hence, a large part of the reason they opted for a civil ceremony during the court battle.

I am happy to say that Paula and Brent are doing well now, and Rosalee has busied herself with smearing Brent and Paula to the rest of the family. Some family members believed her and ostracized them, and others reached out in support to Paula and Brent having been on the receiving end of her antics as well.

"They claim to know God, but
by their actions they deny him.
They are detestable, disobedient and
unfit for doing anything good."

The Bible, Titus 1:16

9

RELIGIOUS ABUSE

Yea, verily, one of the many, many ways that abusers abuse and control and manipulate is by using religion. One of the subcategories of a narcissist that I did not cover in the beginning of this book is the Communal narcissist.

What is a Communal narcissist? Well, it is someone who presents to the community (i.e., society) as someone who is a pillar of the community, pious, righteous, holier than holy, [For those of you old enough to remember, think Jim Bakker *(https://en.wikipedia.org/wiki /Jim_Bakker)*; for those of you not old enough to remember, think about the Catholic sex scandal involving priests and altar boys. *(http://www.cnn. com/2017/06/29/world/timeline-catholic-church-sexual-abuse-scandals/index.html)* But behind closed doors you can bet your sweet bippy that they are cheating on their wives, beating their kids, and probably lying on their taxes. *(http://www.beliefnet. com/faiths/galleries/15-narcissistic-religious-abuse-tactics.aspx?)*

Again, all names and identifying characteristics have been changed in the following case studies.

Frank, age 45, tall, redheaded, outdoorsy type but looks haggard.

Betty, also age 45, bleach blonde, obvious plastic surgery, spray on tan, dressed to impress.

Clients have been married for 25 years and have two grown children. Frank called to try to save their marriage.

Me: "Hey Frank, Hey Betty, how can I help you?"

Frank: "We aren't doing well."

Betty: "I wanted to see a counselor at our church but Frank refused! What is your religion?"

Me: (In my head) "None of your damn business!" (But I knew better.) "I was raised Southern Baptist." (I could tell if I added that I also practice Buddhism she would have shut right down. This seemed to appease her. I had to be very careful about not swearing around this woman as she would get very offended; this actually comes into play later.)

Betty: "Good! We need a Christian counselor to help us and I know you said you swear but I would prefer that you don't!"

Me: "Okay. How can I help you?"

Betty: "Frank is not living up to his potential."

Me: (Raising my eyebrows)

Betty: (Continuing) "When we started having problems, I insisted that Frank come to church with me."

Frank: "I've been going."

Betty: "We did counseling with the pastor at our church but he referred us to you."

Me: (In my head) "Oh shit!" (Knowing that the pastor recognized the need for a higher level of care, which meant psychological issues he could not deal with) "Okay, so what is going on?"

Betty: "He disgusts me."

Frank: (Looking haggard and ashamed, head bowed, not

saying a word)

Me: "Uh, okay, that's a pretty strong statement. What is going on?"

Betty: "He looks at porn!"

Me: "Okay. Frank, how often do you look at porn?" (Trying to determine if there is a sex addiction going on)

Frank: "Just when I want to masturbate."

Betty: (Becoming enraged) "You should NEVER touch yourself! Ever! Every time you do that tells me that I'm not enough for you!"

Frank: "You NEVER want to have sex, and when you do it is when you've been drinking!"

Me: (In my head) "Ah. I see why the pastor referred you." (Before I got a chance to say anything, Betty continued.)

Betty: (Viciously) "That is the only way I can stand to have you touch me!"

Me: "Ok. Stop. Scale of 1 to 10, how interested are you in fixing this relationship?"

Betty: "10! The Lord does not want us to get a divorce! Plus, what would people at church say?"

Frank: (Obviously not on the same page but afraid to voice his true opinion) "Ten." (said with little enthusiasm)

Me: (Starting to get that there was abuse going on.) "When did you first start having problems in your marriage?"

Betty: "With sex and me finding him disgusting? Three years into our marriage."

Me: "How long have you been married?"

Frank: "25 years."

Me: (Frowning) "You waited 22 years to get help?"

Frank: "I asked to go to counseling when she cut me off from sex after the kids were born, but she refused, until this last year."

Betty: "We don't need counseling. We just need to go to church more! Frank wants to separate, but I know God wants us together! God also doesn't approve of your brother or your best friend. I know you're cheating on me with your sister-in-law!"

Frank: "What? No! I am not!"

Betty: (Continuing) "And when you watch television you look at those women on TV, and you want to have sex with them. I know you do. You are evil! You are going to hell!"

Me: "Whoa! Okay, stop. I would like to work with each of you individually for a while before continuing couples counseling."

Betty: (Immediately suspicious) "Why?"

Me: "So I can understand you better and help the relationship."

Betty: "I do not want him talking about me without me being here."

Me: (Recognizing the Machiavellian attempt to control) "Why don't we schedule you first so you'll know how the session will go?"

Betty: (Feeling appeased) "Ok."

I ended the session and scheduled them both for individual sessions as I felt there was more than likely emotional, if not physical, abuse going on. I was right. Sometimes I really hate it when I'm right.

The first session with Betty was very enlightening to say the least.

Me: "Good morning, Betty. So tell me about your family of origin."

Betty: (Already defensive) "What do you mean 'family of origin'?"

Me: (Smiling and being pleasant) "Your mom, your dad, your siblings."

Betty: (Very suspicious) "Why do you need to know about that?"

Me: (Still smiling and pleasant) "It helps me understand your current relationship better."

Betty: (Relaxing just a little) "My mom wanted to be an actress. She worked as a cocktail waitress. My Dad is…(her voice trailed off). My brothers and sisters are wonderful, wonderful, good Christian people! Very successful!"

Me: "So Mom is dead and Dad is still here?"

Betty: "Yes. My mother lived with us until she died two years ago."

Me: "Oh. How did that affect your marriage?"

Betty: (Defensively) "It didn't! I had a duty to take care of her, and I did!"

Me: "How long did she live with you?"

Betty: "For 15 years."

Me: "That's a long time."

Betty went on to explain that her mother was always "sick" and eventually died of cancer. What she described was someone who malingers, in other words, a hypochondriac. The mother was very dramatic and demanding and had no problem spending the family's money on her various illnesses, running to doctors every time she felt she was not getting enough attention, until she really did become terminally ill. The mom was very controlling and very much a victim.

Me: "So tell me about your children."

Betty: "What about them?"

Me: "How are they doing?"

Betty: "I have to do everything for them. They are all children, Frank included!" (Likening the target of abuse to a child in a negative way is a common power tactic that abusers use.) Frank didn't want kids, but I did so I made sure we had them."

Me: (Trying hard not to show any emotion.) "What do you mean?"

Betty: "I poked his condoms with pins. God wanted us to have children. It was the right thing to do. The son of a bitch got fixed after we had our second child."

Me: (I noticed that it was okay for her to swear.) "It sounds like you don't like Frank very much. Does he know you did that? Poked holes in the condoms?"

Betty: "I have to do everything for him. He has no money sense. I am the spiritual leader in the house." (Completely ignoring my question as to whether she ever told him she poked holes in his condoms or why she did not like Frank)

Me: "So what about the sex?"

Betty: "What about it? Men are filthy. Sex is dirty."

Me: "You never told me about your Dad."

Betty: "Daddy drinks too much. He has liver cancer."

Me: "Does he live with you, too?"

Betty: "No. Mom and Daddy got divorced years ago."

Me: "So how did you feel about them divorcing?"

Betty: "He was a cheater and held my mother back from her career. Just like Frank."

Me: "So you feel Frank is holding you back, and you don't like him but you don't want to separate?"

Betty: "He will stay with me because I know what is best for him! He feels so guilty all the time, and he should! Looking at women on TV and masturbating to porn! How dare he! God will punish him."

And so it went. She basically laid out how it was okay for her to treat him poorly because he was masturbating and that her "punishment" of him was what God wanted. Betty clearly had power and control issues. She was very narcissistic and very psychotic. She was what is referred to as a dark triad, which is someone who is Machiavellian (control) narcissistic (i.e., all about them, their wants, their needs, the other person be damned) and psychosis. Betty saw herself as all powerful, and if she couldn't manipulate Frank into staying, she would use the Almighty to do so.

Frank's individual session was equally enlightening. Frank came into the session with pale skin and dark circles under his eyes. He, again, looked like a dog who had been beaten too much. (Not that anyone should ever beat anyone, let alone a dog. But you know what I mean!)

Me: "Hi, Frank! How are you?"

Frank: "I feel awful.'

Me: "Why? What's going on?"

Frank: "Betty kept me up for hours last night screaming at me."

Me: "About?"

Frank: "Coming here. She accused me of having an affair with you."

Me: (In my head) "That's it! I have now officially heard it all" (Outside of my head) "Given that this is your first individual session, that is very interesting. And I don't sleep with my clients by the way. Code of ethics and everything."

Frank: "I know. She's just…This isn't the first time she wouldn't let me sleep. Anytime I have anything important going on, something at work, or a job interview or anything, she picks that night to come in after I've already gone to sleep and pick a fight with me. Last night she demanded that I not talk about her or us to you at all."

Me: "This isn't her session, Frank, it's yours. You can talk about anything you want to."

Frank: "For four hours last night she gave me a sermon on how a man is supposed to be in marriage, and she told me I'm a piece of shit and worthless and that God is disappointed in me."

Me: (In my head) "So she is now the spokesperson for God. Wonder how Gabriel feels about that?"

Frank: (Continuing) "She told me my own dad was disappointed with me."

Me: (Sensing this was important) "Tell me about your family."

Frank: "My mom is married to my step-dad, Sam. He is like a father to me. My real dad died when I was ten of a heart attack."

Me: "Oh Frank, I'm so sorry."

Frank: "He died on my birthday. Betty tells me all the time it was my fault that he died. He was putting up decorations on the ladder, and he just clutched his chest and stumbled off the ladder to the ground. At first I thought he was joking around but then Mom started screaming. By the time the ambulance got there, he was gone."

Me: "It wasn't your fault."

Frank: "She has always been difficult to be with, but when her mother became ill and died, and now her father is dying, she is at church four times a week and rubbing my nose in all my sins. She accuses me of having affairs, of talking about her with family and friends, of not being a good enough Christian. I'm tired. I'm just tired. I just want who she was when we first got together back."

Me: "How was she when you first got together?"

Frank: "She loved sex! She loved doing all the things I liked to do. She was like, well, like me, I guess."

Me: "When did that change?"

Frank: "Pretty much as soon as the wedding ceremony was over."

Me: "How long did you date before you got married?"

Frank: "A little over a year."

Me: "So during the courting phase she was your ideal mate but as soon as you got married she became…?"

Frank: "Hypercritical. I did not want kids. We used protection but we got pregnant, twice. After our youngest, I went and had a vasectomy, for which she has never forgiven me."

You may be wondering why I didn't tell Frank at this point that his wife poked holes in the condoms. It is because of the code of ethics and the HIPPA laws. When I am seeing them as a couple, the couple is the client. When I see them individually, the individual is the client and as such I cannot break confidentiality unless it is a duty to warn situation. So, for example, if Betty had made clear threats about Frank along the lines of "I am going to kill him, and this is how I'm going to do it." Then I would tell Frank so he could protect himself. I would also alert the police.

Frank: (Continuing) "She constantly uses God against me! I don't want to have sex with the women I see on TV, and I only masturbate to porn about once a week!"

Me: "There is nothing wrong with masturbation. That is a completely normal and healthy thing to do."

Frank: "But the Bible…"

Me: "Let me guess, the Bible verse is about not spilling your seed on the ground, yes? Genesis 38:9?"

Frank: "Yes. How did you know?"

Me: "Because the Bible gets misquoted and taken out of context in order to control people all the time. The reason the man in the bible was killed was not because he masturbated, but because he did not impregnate the woman as God commanded. He defied God. That is why he was punished, not the masturbation part."

I must say, I wish they would have prepared us more in our training in theology. You would be amazed at the number of times I have had to counter an abuser using the Bible as the excuse for their abuse. Fortunately, I have many friends who are priests, shamans, etc., in many different religions that I consult with when one of these events happens.

Frank: "How do you know that for sure?"

Me: "I talk to religious leaders about questions clients have, and that is one of the common ones."

Frank: (Looking relieved, sighing) "That's good to know. What about the porn?"

Me: "Honestly? I am not a huge fan of porn because I think it distorts what is normal for both a male and female body. However, if you are not attracted to your partner and you are not having normal sexual relations, I can understand the use of porn to masturbate in moderation."

Frank: "She tells me I'm ugly and disgusting all the time because I use porn. She also says that it is an insult to her."

Me: "But she doesn't see that she is insulting you saying that to you?"

Frank: "No. Everything is my fault, according to her. I just want her to be happy."

Me: "How about yourself? Do you deserve to be happy?"

Frank: (After a long pause) "Sometimes I think so, and sometimes I think I deserve how she treats me. She is such a pillar of the community. Everybody loves her at our church."

I would like to point out here that often with communal narcissists the mask is different between church and home. Outstanding citizen in public, horrific abuser in private. *(https://www.psychologytoday.com/blog/tech-support/201605/the-communal-narcissist-another-wolf-wearing-sheep-outfit)*

Me: "I think working on your self-esteem will help you a lot. I would like you to get The Self- Esteem Workbook by Schiraldi. Also, I want you to get The Disease to Please by Harriet Braiker. You are 100% responsible for your own happiness. She is 100% responsible for her own happiness. You are not responsible for her happiness."

This statement appeared to be a shocker for him.

Frank: "She tells me all the time I am the reason she is so unhappy."

Me: "Nope. Each person is responsible for their own happiness, and if they are that unhappy being with someone else, the kindest thing to do is to move on."

Frank had a hard time wrapping his head around that. He was a people pleaser to the nth degree. He thought he had found his perfect mate in Betty because she liked all the things he liked and did all the things he liked to do. What he did not realize is that Betty was simply mirroring him so she could get her hooks into him. Once she did, the devalue and discard began. When she sensed that he may leave is when she began poking holes in his condoms so that he would be forced to stay with her out of obligation, although she claimed it was because "God wanted them to procreate!" Betty only came to individual counseling two more times. Frank came a few more times, but he was not strong enough to stand up to Betty. Every time after he came to therapy when he got home, she would interrogate him and demand to know what we talked about and what was said. I told him to answer that we are working on self-esteem, which was true. He would do that but then she would later that night fly into a rage and keep him up demanding to know "The Truth." It was easier for him to give in to his abuser than to face the prospect of confrontation and leaving, especially since she was bombarding him with guilt and God. Unfortunately, he was not done being abused.

Abusers absolutely do not want their target to work on self-esteem. Why? Because they know that once the target starts getting strong and understanding that no one deserves to be screamed at, raged at, deprived of sleep, told that God hates them, etc., the abuser will have lost the power of control over them. Abusers will often therapist shop, trying to find a therapist that will see their world view; if they cannot find one that agrees with them and their abuse, they will declare that all therapists are hacks and refuse to go to therapy and stop their partner, their target, from going to therapy.

Conversely, abusers will also use the opposite of God to control their target of abuse. Again, all names and identifying characteristics have been changed.

James, age 33, tall, handsome, a writer by profession, and suffering from depression.

> **Me:** "Hey Jim! How are you? What would you like to work on today?"

> **James:** (Looking just sad) "I feel so lonely."

> **Me:** "Tell me more."

> **James:** "I mean, I'm in a relationship and I love her, but…"

Me: "But...?"

James: "I started dating Natalie, and my friends didn't like her so I stopped hanging out with those friends and started hanging out with her friends."

Me: (Seeing the red flag immediately) "Oh."

James: "Her friends are into some pretty weird stuff. One of them considers herself a black witch."

Me: "Okay."

James: "So Natalie wanted my friends to like her, and she tried too hard. When my friends didn't respond the way she wanted, she insisted I not hang out with them."

Me: "You realize that is a red flag, right?"

James: "Yeah. I guess. I mean, well, I was maintaining some of my friendships, and when I wanted to spend time with one of my female friends, well, Natalie called her."

Me: "And?"

James: "She tried to pick a fight with my friend."

Me: "Yikes!"

James: "Constance and I have been friends for almost a decade. Connie said she refused to fight with Natalie but Natalie said that Connie said all sorts of things to her. I defended Natalie instead of Connie."

Me: "How long have you been dating Natalie?"

James: "Less than a year."

Me: "So what happened?"

James: "Connie and I are no longer speaking."

Me: "So let me understand. You and Constance had been friends for almost a decade. Had she ever lied to you or given you any reason to not believe her?"

James: (Clearly struggling with the gaslighting) "No. She was a good friend. She never lied to me but Natalie keeps saying that she wants me sexually and that she is just jealous of our relationship."

Me: "Tell me more about Constance."

James: "She is also a writer. She and her husband, David, have a really good relationship."

Me: "So in the almost 10 years you've known her, has she ever made a move on you?"

James: (Again struggling because of the gaslighting) "No. But she has told me that she finds me attractive and that she is sure that we were together in a past life somewhere. Natalie came unglued when I told her that, and she said that Constance wants me and that I have to stop her when she is affectionate with me."

Me: "What do you mean affectionate?"

James: "She would hug me and hold my hand when we did stuff together. I never thought it was romantic until Natalie came unglued. Natalie said it was sensual and that I should stop. She said that Connie was sexually harassing me."

Me: "Natalie sounds very insecure. Did you have uncomfortable feelings before Natalie suggested to you that your friend's affection was wrong?"

James: (Again struggling) "No."

At this point I need to explain bonding and oxytocin again. Abusers instinctively know that if the target of abuse is making skin to skin contact, there is oxytocin being released. That is our "bonding" or "love" chemical. It is similar to dopamine, and it gets released when we do anything pleasurable such as touch, hug, riding a roller coaster, or having sex. Abusers isolate their victim and are again morbidly jealous, wanting to be the ONLY source of bonding, so they will demand that the target of abuse be isolated from physical touch as well as isolating them emotionally. They want to be the ONLY source of physical touch for them so that the target of abuse is completely dependent upon them for everything from physical to emotional to comfort to financial matters. Because abusers are inherently jealous and very, very insecure, they use the jealousy to make sure no one "touches" their property and yes, they view their targets as property, not people.

James only came in a few times and then stopped coming. I was pretty sure it was because Natalie insisted he stop coming.

Two months later James's brother came to see me.

Larry, age 29, tall, good-looking, and intelligent coming in for anxiety.

Me: "Hey Larry. How are you? How can I help you today?"

Larry: "I know you were seeing my brother James."

Me: (In my head) "Christ almighty! I wish people understood the HIPPA laws!" (Outside my head) "Larry, due to the privacy laws known as HIPPA, I can neither confirm nor deny that I have seen anybody. I hope you understand."

Larry: "Yeah. I get it. It's okay. I know you can't say

anything. My anxiety is for my brother. He isn't doing well."

Me: "Okay. What is going on?"

Larry: "This woman that he is dating is evil. She has managed to isolate him from family and friends. When he is with us and if anybody says anything about her, he clearly runs back and tells her our concerns, and then she won't let him hang out with us anymore. I've lost my brother. I'm just sick about it, and I don't know what to do."

Me: "Larry, if he is an adult (because remember I can't even let on that I know anything about the brother), there is nothing you can do except speak the truth, be supportive, and do not play her game."

Larry: "He has changed for the worst. He used to be happy and social and funny and just a great older brother. Now he is smoking and drinking and just, well, mean. His sense of humor has gotten just nasty. She puts him down, subtly, and then he denies that she puts him down. When we were out with the family he made a joke; she shot him a dirty look and said something nasty under her breath to him. I could tell by the look on his face. Kris, they had been dating less than a month at that point! He got rid of his best friend because Natalie was jealous of her!"

Me: (Sighing) Larry, all you can do is remind him he deserves to be treated with respect. If you push too hard, he will do what I call a 'Romeo and Juliet' or the "backfire effect."

Larry: "What do you mean?"

Me: "I mean that usually the ego would rather be 'right' than admit it made a mistake. People who have chosen either the initial abuser or another abusive relationship will dig their heels in to prove that the person they are with is 'good' even when all evidence points to the solid fact that the person is an abuser." (https://www.psychologytoday.com/blog/confessions-techie/201008/dump-your-ego; see also https://www.psychologytoday.com/blog/the-wise-open-mind/201007/what-are-the-limitations-your-ego-mind) "Much like Romeo and Juliet, staying together despite family and friends warning them against each other, to their own demise."

Larry: "Yeah. I can see that."

Me: "It isn't a mature response, but it is an ego response. It is flawed logic. Much like when an abused person says, 'Well, I've invested a lot of time in this so I should stay.' If a money investment stopped paying, would you keep putting money into it?"

Larry: "No! Of course not."

Me: "But a person with CPTSD will. They will stay long after the love that has been put in has stopped being returned."

Larry: "But that wasn't how he was before he started dating Natalie. It's like, it's like, I don't know him anymore!"

Me: "I know, hon. I know. This is the hardest part of watching someone you love allow themselves to be changed and destroyed by an abuser."

I encouraged him to read The Disease to Please by Harriet Braiker and any and all articles he could find on emotional abuse. He came into my office about once a month to vent and to discuss the latest interaction with his brother and the girlfriend.

Me: "Hey Larry how are you doing?"

Larry: "Not good. So Natalie was trying to impress our

sister Martha. Natalie showed her the black magic alter in her apartment and then told her she was casting spells over our brother to make him stay with her. Martha was terrified. We were all raised Christian."

Me: "Wow."

Larry: "I started reading up on black magic and spells and how the victim behaves. Kris, it is EXACTLY what is happening to James! Martha told me that Natalie insinuated she was also casting spells against me and Mom and Dad since we don't like her."

Me: "Wow."

Larry: "What do we do?"

Me: (Thinking in my head) "They so never prepared me for this in grad school." (Outside my head) "I am not a spiritual advisor, and I know nothing about the dark arts nor do I really want to. However, I would suggest going to your pastor or priest and talking that part of it over with him or her."

Larry: "Okay. I will."

You have to meet the client where they are, and where Larry was, was desperate to find an explanation for why his older brother had such a radical change in personality. Larry was not schizotypal in which belief in paranormal and superstitions is one of the hallmarks of that disorder, which is also not to say that people who believe or have experiences in the paranormal are mentally ill. He truly believed what his sister Martha had reported and, based on his Christian belief system, it was entirely possible that the abuser was indeed practicing black magic on his brother and the family and friends. I encouraged him to seek out guidance from his religion. I also told him that there is such a thing as free will and no amount of black magic can negate that and to not be afraid. He seemed to take comfort in that.

Why would this person go out of their way to tell a family member about the alter and the spell casting? Intimidation. Wanting to control through fear: "Do what I want or I will hex you!" The very flip side of using Christianity and God to control. Same end, different means. Plus, Larry reported that Martha was into the paranormal, somewhat of a goth, and more than likely the abuser, Natalie, felt she would have an ally with her to the family. Last I heard, no one in the family was speaking to Natalie. Larry had asked his church to start a prayer chain for James to protect him from black magic. James was still in the abusive relationship. It is unknown if James was aware that his girlfriend was practicing black magic. His family believed that if he did know he would have left her because even though he wasn't "as religious" he was still spiritual and would not have put up with that. But given the complete sway she had over him, who knows!

"If you are an approval addict, your behaviour
is as easy to control as that of any other junkie.
All a manipulator need do is a simple two-step process:
Give you what you crave, and then threaten to take it away.
Every drug dealer in the world plays this game."

**Harriet B. Braiker,
Who's Pulling Your Strings?
How to Break the Cycle of
Manipulation and Regain
Control of Your Life**

TOTALLY ADDICTED TO ATTACHMENT STYLES?

I often hear targets of abuse say how "addicted" to their abuser they are or were. They are correct. When leaving an abuser you have to treat the abuser as if they were a substance and you are leaving the substance. "What?" you say. "What the hell are you talking about?" I'm talking about being psychologically AND physically addicted to someone, just like an addict is addicted to their drug of choice so, too, the target to the abuser. (Counseling Today, July 17, volume 60: 26 – 29; Neurocounseling: Bridging Brain and Behavior by Justin Jacques) When family members and friends try to intercede and help the abused, they—the abused—often become angry and defensive. Why? Because just like with a substance abuse addict, they are angry that you are suggesting they need to quit their favorite drug of choice. They are happy with you as long as you are enabling them and angry with you when you point out that the drug of choice is slowly killing them. So how does this addiction happen? Let me break this down for you by describing the cycle of abuse.

The abuser targets the target and sets their sights on them. They get together with the target and begin the "honeymoon" phase or the "love bombing" phase. In this phase the abuser spends as much time with the target as humanly possible. Every free moment they are either with them, texting them, IMing them, calling them, or otherwise. While bombarding them with their presence, the abuser will start to mirror to the target all the things the target wishes for in a relationship. The target likes opera? Why, guess what? So does the abuser! The target always wanted to travel the world? Why, guess what? So does the abuser! The target likes chocolate? Why, guess what? So does the abuser! The abused target of the love bombing begins releasing a ridiculous amount of feel good chemicals including oxytocin, endorphins, dopamines, etc.

"But," you say, "hang on a minute! How do you tell if it is love bombing or if you are just really well matched?" Here is a clue: Even people who are well matched do not have EXACTLY the same likes and dislikes and are not afraid to be different or disagree; they also don't spend every waking minute together nor do they text constantly and/or demand constant contact, either in person or through electronic means. The abuser will change their opinion in order to be like the person they want to be with. But then during the discard phase their true opinion will emerge, and they will make the target feel wrong for liking something they don't really like. Sound crazy? It is.

Let me continue and really blow your mind. Now they are showering the target with compliments, time, attention, gifts, etc, but over the top type of thing, not the normal "Hey, I really like you and here is what is neat about you" but the literal "You're so awesome! You're so wonderful! We are so much alike. You're my soulmate/twin flame/meant to be." So the abuser now has the target bamboozled that they are "the perfect boyfriend or perfect girlfriend," everything the target has been longing for in a relationship. Here is where it gets nasty for the target of abuse: Because of the constant love bombing and the constant physical contact, usually sex, the target of abuse is now intoxicated with the oxytocin, dopamines, serotonin, and other feel good chemicals Once the target commits to the abuser, the abuser's mask starts slipping and the demands start: "Get rid of your friends," "I don't want you working with that coworker," "I want you to quit your job," "I don't like your family," "How dare you have a girls or guys night out!" The abuser starts in with the intermittent positive rewards. In other words, where there was constant praise, it now happens only once in a while. Where there was sex galore, you are lucky if you get it once a month, and as the abuser devalues and discards, the poor target starts producing oxytocin like crazy in an effort to get the abuser to start "love bombing" them again. *(https:// www.psychologytoday.com/blog/the-athletes-way/201705/face-face-connectedness-oxytocin-and-your-vagus-nerve; see also https://www.psychologytoday.com/blog/reading-between-the-headlines/201703/love-bombing-have-you-ever-been-the-target)*

Then once the target of abuse has met as many of the abuser's demands as possible, the abuser begins raging at all hours of the day or night. The abuser will text constantly and demand an immediate response to the texts or IMs; if ignored, that will be fuel for the next rage session. The abuser will become irrationally jealous, and if family and friends are still in the picture, the abuser will begin to lie and gaslight and demand that the target believe their smear campaign as compared to how the family and friend really are. They will also demand that the target of abuse tell the abuser EVERYTHING that is said or happens when they are not present. So, in other words, the target goes out and has lunch with a family member or friend, the abuser will demand to know everything. NO SECRETS! They will guilt trip the abused into revealing private conversations, especially ones that family members have in an effort to bring the abused back to sanity and acknowledge the abuse. At this point the target of abuse will begin to have serious cognitive dissonance and not be able to resolve what the abuser is telling them versus what is reality and, in an effort to resolve that discomfort, get rid of the remaining family or friends. Now the target of abuse is completely isolated from all or almost all family and friends and is only allowed to have friends the abuser approves (i.e., their own flying monkeys). So now the abuse begins in earnest. The target can do nothing right. The abuser gets narcissistic supply from watching the target of abuse twist themselves into a pretzel trying to please them. Family and friends stand by helplessly as they watch their loved one's memory and health start to fail them. The abused have dark circles under their eyes from the lack of sleep. They have no support network since the abuser demanded that they give up any family members or friends who saw through the abuser's mask. Their memory starts slipping more and more as they live in a constant state of survival mode, and the CPTSD symptoms kick in. The nightly rages, the irrational arguments, the gaslighting, the inability to resolve the cognitive dissonance—all contribute to the brain being unable to place short-term memory into long-term memory. Abuse amnesia sets in. Questioning their sanity sets in. They will ask themselves, "Am I crazy? Did I really say that? Didn't that really happen?"

Hopefully, at some point the target will get tired of the nightly rages, the putdowns, the drama, and want to leave. But just when you, as the family member or the friend, are hopeful that FINALLY this time the target of abuse will leave, the abuser does an about-face and "Hoovers," meaning the abuser literally sucks the target of abuse back into the cycle of abuse, like a vacuum cleaner, with the promise of change and begins to love bomb the target. This causes the target of abuse to feel immense relief as the feel good chemicals—oxytocin, dopamine, endorphins—flood the target's system again and they get that "high." Only this time, the love bombing lasts only long enough to get the target of abuse back into the relationship, and then the devalue and discard and raging and abuse starts at an accelerated rate. Each time the target thinks that at last the abuser loves them and sees them, but each time the abuser abuses them, mentally, emotionally and eventually, physically. *(Psychology Today, June 2017; Poison People by Katherine Schreiber, 50 – 58; 88)* The inconsistency, the intermittent positive rewards, and the flooding of the system with feel good chemicals make the target of abuse as addicted to the drama and abuse as a drug addict is addicted to meth or heroin or alcohol.

The most susceptible people to abuse are those with a childhood history of neglect and abuse. In a misguided attempt to heal the original or core wound with the parent or caregiver, they seek out relationships in which the abuse or neglect is played out again. But instead of healing the wound, they compound the wound over and over and over and create more and more shame for themselves.

So what exactly am I talking about? I am talking about attachment styles. "What the heck is an attachment style?" you ask. It is how we were emotionally attached to our caregivers. There are four attachment styles: Secure, Anxious/Preoccupied, Fearful/Avoidant, and Dismissive/Avoidant.

If a child has a Secure attachment style and is loved and feels safe in his/her environment, the child grows up to be a secure adult unlikely to put up with abuse for long if at all. If, however, the attachment to the caregiver was insecure, touch and go, not safe, inconsistent, and had episodes of intermittent positive rewards, which caused the child to feel anxious, that child has been groomed and is much more likely to be abused or put up with abuse because it feels familiar to them, because it mimics the attachment to the caregiver in childhood. The Anxious/Preoccupied attachment style is the narcissist's feast. They are more likely to have drama-filled relationships; need validation, which leaves them vulnerable to love bombing; and have an aversion to being alone, which fits in perfectly with the narcissist needing to be with them every waking moment in the love bombing phase.

If there was abuse with the caregiver, the child will have a Fearful/Avoidant attachment, meaning they struggle with intimate relationships and have few close friends. A person with a Fearful/Avoidant attachment style is unlikely to get involved with an abuser. The last attachment style, however, is where you will find most of abusers. The Dismissive/Avoidant attachment style avoids true intimacy and will avoid ANY emotional obligation or responsibility. They will have many "acquaintances" but no truly close friends. They will be passive/aggressive and/or narcissistic. *(https://www.psychologytoday.com/blog/communication-success/201507/what-is-your-relationship-attachment-style)*

So, is a target of abuse doomed to addiction to the abuse and the abuser because of the attachment style? No. Attachment styles can and do change. A person with a secure attachment style after having been abused by a malignant narcissist or malignant borderline will, for a time, have an insecure attachment style as a result of having been abused. A person with an insecure attachment style will benefit from surrounding themselves with good friends who are trustworthy and by involving themselves with romantic partners who have a secure attachment style. They, too, will become more secure. Peers and romantic partners can and do influence adult attachment styles. Hang out with secure and mature friends and you will become more secure and mature. Hang out with insecure and immature friends and you, too, will find yourself becoming less and less secure and more immature. Who you hang out with is who you will begin acting like. *(https://www.psychologytoday.com/blog/the-mysteries-love/201502/attachment-styles-cant-change-can-they)*

Shame comes into play with attachment styles and addiction. If a person has a secure attachment, it is unlikely they will have or be susceptible to shame in their adult lives. When a target of abuse has had an insecure attachment style and is shamed a lot in childhood, either by the caregiver or by the mistaken belief that the caregiver's absence or neglect or abuse or intermittent positive rewards is somehow their own doing, that person will grow up and harbor a great deal of deep-seated shame, which an abuser such as a malignant narcissist or a malignant borderline will feed on and expand on by continuing the insecure attachment with verbal abuse, gaslighting, the cold shoulder and, in some cases, physical attacks. The abuser makes sure to tell the target that any and everything is wrong with them and that the abuser's unhappiness is all the target's fault, which increases the sense of shame that the target has. Targets start having cognitive dissonance, and their thinking becomes more and more flawed. They will often say things like "But I've invested so much time into this relationship; it would be stupid to leave now." At which point I ask them the money investment question of "If a money investment stopped paying you a return, would you keep investing?" The answer is always a no, and then I will point out the incongruency in thinking differently about a relationship time investment. In addition to the altered thinking because of the abuse, now you have the flip side of not leaving. Targets know on some level they should leave the abuse but because of ego, mistaken thoughts and beliefs (time invested fallacy), attachment style (believing that no one will ever love them and they will die alone), or low self-esteem, they stay, sometimes for years, sometimes forever. Only when they decide that, like an alcoholic, they have hit rock bottom and they do not want to feel this way anymore do targets of abuse seem to finally decide to leave. *(Counseling Today, May 2017, 59 (11): 24 – 31; Becoming Shameless by Laurie Meyers)*

Let me illustrate by giving two case studies of attachment style and shame. Again, all identifying names and characteristics have been changed.

Jason, age 40, married, no kids. Dealing with anxiety from a narcissistic boss from hell. Came in to get coping strategies.

Me: "Hey Jason! So what are we working on today?"

Jason: "I hate my job."

Me: "You hate what you do or you hate the people you work with?" (Trying to determine what the issue is because one is very different from the other in terms of counseling)

Jason: "I hate my boss. He is a total douchebag."

Me: "Oh dear. Tell me more."

Jason went on to describe a very dysfunctional work

environment in which the boss promoted his flying monkeys, was an alcoholic, drank on the job, encouraged pettiness and nastiness among the coworkers, stole ideas and took credit for them, and those were just the highlights. The worst of it was that the boss needed a scapegoat, and because Jason obviously didn't like the guy, he was it.

Jason: "I just feel demoralized when I get home. He will yell at me for no reason in front of the entire staff."

Me: "Why are you staying?"

Jason: "I need the money."

Me: "What does your wife say about all this?"

Jason: "She tells me I should leave."

Me: "But you don't want to leave because…"

Jason: "It pays really well."

Me: "Tell me about your family.

Jason: "My mom and dad split when I was five. Dad is an alcoholic."

Me: "Huh."

Jason: "What has my family got to do with my job?"

Me: "Did your dad yell at you a lot when you were a kid?"

Jason: "He would yell at Mom and me a lot. That's why they divorced. I didn't see much of him after that."

Me: "Do you think you deserved that? To be yelled at when you were little?"

Jason: "No."

Me: "Do you think you deserve to be yelled at by your boss?"

Jason: "No."

Me: "So why do you subject yourself to it? What are you hoping will change?"

The light started coming on in Jason's brain as he put together the early childhood attachment style of anxious attachment style and how his boss reminded him of his dad. His attachment style had become more secure as he matured and married his wife, who had a secure attachment style. But being in the presence of an abuser, and an active alcoholic who reminded him of his dad, threw him back into the old ways of thinking that somehow maybe magically the boss/dad would see how good he was for the company and that everything would be okay. This occurred over the course of several months of therapy. Finally, he got it!

Me: "Hey Jason! What are we working on today?"

Jason: "I quit my job because I got hired by a different company!"

Me: "Huzzah! What happened?"

Jason: "Harold showed up drunk after lunch and tried to start screaming at me again, and I just picked up my jacket and walked out. I contacted a headhunter and started interviewing that week. It was scary as hell but, with my wife's encouragement, I left. No one should have to put up with that!"

Me: "Good job!"

Jason had an insecure attachment style as a child that became more secure but was made insecure again after being confronted with an abusive boss. His wife had a secure attachment style; she encouraged him, literally gave him courage, to see he didn't deserve to be screamed at and to leave and find another job. During our time together we worked on self-esteem and correcting the mistaken thoughts and beliefs that Jason's wounded inner child had about himself in regards to his Dad and his boss. Jason got into the other job and at last contact was doing well.

Now here is an insecure attachment style with no encouragement and lots of shame.

Stacy, age 38, in a same-sex relationship, works at a call center, and is coming in for depression.

Me: "Hey Stacy! How can I help you today?"

Stacy: "I just feel so depressed."

Me: "What's going on?"

Stacy: "I can't do anything right. I'm 38, and I hate my life. I don't have any friends, and my partner, Natasha, tells me I can't do anything right. She told me I needed to get counseling."

Me: (Already sensing a red flag) "Tell me more."

Stacy: "Tash and I got together a year ago. It was a whirlwind romance; she swept me off my feet. We moved in together within two months. Everything was amazing at first but now…"

Me: "You feel devalued and discarded?"

Stacy: "Yes! I asked her to come to counseling with me but she said she didn't need it."

Me: "Tell me about your family of origin."

Stacy: "My mom died when I was 8. My dad didn't get me

into counseling; he sent me to a psychiatrist and put me on a bunch of pills. He moved me and my sister around a lot. We never got to really settle anywhere. And also, you know, I'm a lesbian so I had to deal with all of that."

Me: "How did your family respond to your sexuality?"

Stacy: "My dad came unglued and said I was going to hell. Both he and his mom pretty much disowned me. My mom's mom seemed to be only just okay with it."

Me: "So did they make you feel wrong?"

Stacy: "Oh God, yes! I had religion thrown in my face. They were embarrassed to let other family members know. I don't have any close friends. Tash was the first person to really want to get to know me."

Me: "So tell me about your relationship."

Stacy: "Tash wanted to spend all her time with me, and she used to text me all the time. She would tell me how amazing I am. It felt wonderful. Like everything I ever wanted from my family but couldn't get."

Me: "When did it change?"

Stacy: "After we moved in together. I suddenly couldn't do anything right. I wasn't making enough money, I wasn't helping out enough around the house. I was suddenly not pleasing her in bed. My ideas were laughed at. She told me I could make way more money at my job if I just lied."

Me: "What do you do for a living?"

Stacy: "I work a call center sales job. There is the potential to make a lot of money, and some people do. But I don't know. Lying just isn't my thing, but Tash keeps telling me I could be making six figures a year if I just loosen up and lie."

Me: "You realize that lying is NEVER a good idea, right?"

Stacy: "Tash tells me that everybody lies. Even counselors."

Me: (In my head) "Mutherfucker projection! Of course she did!" (Outside my head) "Hon, I do not lie to my clients. Good counselors don't. To lie would be to undermine the therapeutic process, and as far as everyone lying goes, there are white lies and then there is gaslighting."

Stacy: "What's the difference? Tash says all lies are the same."

Me: (In my head) "So the abuser is already setting up the conflict. If I disagree, the client will go home and tell her what I said and then the abuser, Tash, will begin the leveling." (Outside my head) "Let me explain the difference."

I went on to explain the difference between lying to save someone's feelings, a white lie, and gaslighting and outright lying, which is done to save the liar's ego. I also need to explain leveling. What an abuser will do is try to convince the target of abuse that they know as much or more than any counselor. They will use and misuse psychological terms in an effort to convince the target that they know what they are talking about and to bring the counselor down to their level. They will attempt to convince the target of abuse that the counselor does not have the expertise or knowledge that they do in psychology. It is an abuse technique known as leveling. And that is EXACTLY what Tasha did.

On our next visit, Stacy was distant and suspicious, asking and reasking questions about lying and other psychological issues.

Me: "Stacy, you seem out of sorts. What is going on?"

Stacy: "I told Tash everything we talked about in our

session. She said you are a bad counselor and you don't know what you are talking about. She said again that everybody lies."

Me: "Hm. That's interesting. What do you think?" (I was not about to play the abuser's game. Abusers want the counselor to defend themselves because then when the target of abuse goes back and tells them, the abuser knows they have the counselor's Achilles' heel.)

Stacy: "You seem to know what you are talking about. You seem to be telling me the truth."

Me: "Why do you think Tash wanted you to doubt my abilities or make you believe I was lying to you?"

Stacy: (Becoming upset) "I don't know! When I get back from seeing you, she demands to know everything we talked about!"

Me: "You have a right to privacy. You don't have to tell her everything if you don't want to."

Stacy: (Again upset) "Tash says that is lying by omission if I don't tell her everything, especially anything that is said about her by either of us."

Me: "No. That is not lying by omission. That is you having your session be your session."

Stacy: "Tasha and I yell a lot at each other. She says that drama is normal in a relationship. That she criticizes me because she loves me. When I make a point, she calls me names and then stops talking to me, sometimes for days at a time, until I apologize to her for making her mad."

Me: (Raising my eyebrows) "No, Stacy. Drama and yelling are absolutely NOT normal in a healthy relationship. Disagreements are normal but there should never be any yelling or name calling or unconstructive criticism or stonewalling or contempt or defensiveness."

Stacy: "Really?"

Me: "Yes. Really. Healthy relationships have good communication, respect, openness, constructive criticism, a willingness to see the other's point of view and compromise."

Stacy: (Frowning) "Oh."

John Gottman proved that point over and over again. *(https://www.gottman.com/blog/the-four-horsemen-recognizing-criticism-contempt-defensiveness-and-stonewalling/)* Stacy never had a good role model for what a healthy relationship looked like and because of her insecure attachment style would become anxious when her abuser Tasha stonewalled so she would end up apologizing for arguments that were not her fault. We worked more on self-esteem and attachment style issues for the rest of the session. The next week her abuser, Tash, pulled out all stops.

Me: "Hey Stacy, how are you?"

Stacy: "I think this will be my last session."

Me: "Okay. What's going on?"

Stacy: "Tash says that by me talking about her and my relationship with her that I am triangulating."

Me: (In my head) "Oh for fuck sake!" (Outside of my head) "No, honey, that is not triangulating. You have a right to talk about whatever you want to and whoever you want to in a counseling session. Triangulating is when you bring a third party into a conversation and put words in that person's mouth such as "so and so said such and such about you" when, in fact, so and so never said such and such. That is triangulating."

Stacy: "She says you are trying to break us up."

Me: (Frowning) "Do you feel like I'm trying to break you up?"

Stacy: (Struggling with the cognitive distortion and dissonance) "No. I tell her everything we talk about in our session. I mean. We've been working on self-esteem, but when I go home to work on the workbook, Tash interrupts me and says the mirror work is childish and stupid."

Me: "What do you think?"

Stacy: (Very quietly) "I liked the mirror work and the workbook."

Me: "Then keep doing it."

That was the last time I saw Stacy. She called and cancelled the next appointment because her abuser, Tasha, didn't like the way the counseling was going even though I never once said anything about Tasha; but I did assert my being the expert, which Tasha did not like. Tasha also did not like the idea of her target getting healthy self-esteem and a good attachment style. If Stacy had been willing to stop telling Tasha everything that was said in our session and work on her self-esteem and attachment issues, she would have clearly seen the manipulation and control that Tasha exerted over her and left the relationship. Tasha knew that so, therefore, interfered with the counseling process. Stacy was more afraid of losing the illusion of Tasha, the love bombing that occurred in the beginning of the relationship, than she was of being controlled and manipulated and lied to by Tasha once the love bombing phase was over. She wasn't healthy enough to tell Tasha to back off and let her go to counseling without having to tell her "everything."

"Toxic people manipulate two types of helpers to do their dirty work against a victim, innocent people who don't see the abuse and people who purposefully ignore the abuse."

Shannon Thomas

ABUSE BY PROXY AND PARENTAL ALIENATION

"What is abuse by proxy?" Believe it or not, I've been giving examples of it throughout this book. Whenever an abuser uses someone else like a flying monkey, or the court system, or the target of abuse, to harass, level, or harm another, it is abuse by proxy. Occasionally, the target is the one relaying the abuse to family and friends (i.e., when the target speaks just exactly like the abuser to the family and friends). I will give a more detailed case study in a moment. Right now I want to talk about one of the most insidious uses of abuse by proxy: parental alienation.

Parental alienation occurs when someone leaves the abuser and there are children involved. Remember, abusers cannot tolerate losing in any way, shape, or form so when their favorite emotional and/or physical punching bag finally leaves them, they become enraged. When a divorce occurs, there are children involved, and one of the parents has a malignant personality disorder, you can predict pretty accurately that the parent with the personality disorder will A. Fight the divorce. B. Demand reconciliation and/or reunification therapy. C. Fight over every last material item. D. Demand full custody. E. Drag the other parent back to court yearly until the child reaches adulthood or can tell the courts to please stop on their behalf. F. Bad-mouth the parent who is leaving the abuser, and/or G. All of the above. When a target of abuse leaves an abuser and there are children involved, the best you can do is to parallel parent, not co parent, and the abuser will do all they can to smear the target of abuse to the kids. That is parental alienation. Both sexes engage in this heinous behavior without regard for what it is doing psychologically to their own children. Their end goal is to have the kids hate and abuse the target of abuse. *(https://www. psychologytoday.com/blog/caught-between-parents /201203/ domestic-violence-proxy-getting-it-right-and-getting-it-wrong)*

As I have mentioned before, most therapists have not been trained in what personality disorders are, let alone the toll the malignant ones take on the target of abuse. When a divorce is happening, the abuser will attempt to bankrupt the target of abuse, prevent them from having legal counsel, and manipulate and/or try to charm the socks off of any court-mandated counselor and the judge, if they can. When charm doesn't work, they will resort to the victim stance and crocodile tears. When that doesn't work, the abuser will then use any and all flying monkeys they can to achieve their end goal of hurting the target of abuse by taking the kids away from them emotionally and making the child or children believe that the target of abuse is really the bad guy. If they can wrest custody from the target or get more than 50/50, they then feel they have financial control over the target as well. For abusers of all types, it is all about control. If they cannot force you to stay in the relationship, they will make you pay in more ways than one.

Perpetrators of parental alienation are both male and female, malignant borderline, malignant narcissist, or sociopath or dark triad. They pretend to care about the well-being of the child or children involved but, in reality, it is all about getting and maintaining control. If they cannot they will smear the other parent, the one who left to the courts, the family, and friends and worst to their own child or children, and then proceed to use the kids as pawns in their own sick power play.

Let me give you a case study example.

Ulie, age 55, widowed, didn't want to be alone so he got onto a dating website and immediately got hooked by his soon-to-be-ex Esther, who was 15 years younger than Ulie. They had one child together, a girl, age 4, named Darla. Esther began demanding Ulie give up his family and friends, and was jealous of his coworkers, and after the birth of Darla cut him off from sex. They were married five years; he started counseling to work on his marriage. Esther refused to come to couples counseling so Ulie filed for divorce.

Me: "Hey Ulie! So what are we working on today?"

Ulie: "Esther is bad-mouthing me to Darla. Darla has started to act weird around me. Like withdrawn. She finally said that 'Mommy said you,' meaning me, 'was a bad, bad man.'

Me: "Oh dear. How did you handle it?"

Ulie: "I said 'No, honey. I'm not a bad man.'"

Me: "Ok. What did she say?"

Ulie: "She said that 'Mommy said you would say that and that I shouldn't believe you. But I want to.' And then she changed the subject and asked me for a grilled cheese sandwich."

Me: "Oh dear. Well, it sounds like she doesn't entirely believe her mother about you."

Ulie: "No, not right now. But I know that every time she is with her mother that woman is bad- mouthing me, and I know my soon-to-be-ex-mother-in-law is doing the same thing."

Me: "All you can do is keep reminding her that you love her and never, and I mean never, bad- mouth her mom or her grandmother to her."

Ulie: "How do I protect myself? How do I protect her?"

Me: "Actions always speak louder than words. She already doesn't believe what her mom is telling her because she sees that by your actions, you love her. Just keep reassuring her that you are there for her and keep the line of communication open."

As the divorce progressed, Esther upped her antics from changing pickup and dropoff times and places and then telling Darla that "Daddy wasn't there because he didn't love her" to sending her over to Ulie's with no shoes or supplies so he would be forced to buy new ones. When he didn't, Esther would again tell Darla that "Daddy didn't love her." If Ulie instead bought supplies and shoes at the Salvation Army or Goodwill, then Esther would say that "Daddy didn't think she was worth new shoes or new supplies." This woman was truly a piece of work.

Meanwhile, Darla, being just a little over four years old, was caught in the middle of this insanity. Esther started using guilt trips on the little girl, demanding that she love her more than her father. Darla started acting out when she came over to her father's.

Me: "Hey Ulie. How is it going?"

Ulie: "Darla is not doing well. I get her back from Esther, and it is like I have to reinstruct her on how to behave."

Me: "That isn't uncommon. What is she doing?"

Ulie: "Well, she starts sassing me a lot and seems very angry, even though I haven't done anything."

Me: "That is because you are the safer target. If she expressed anger with her mother or toward her mother, what would Esther do?"

Ulie: "Come unglued."

Me: "Exactly. In a way, this is good because this means you feel safer to her. However, and this is a big however, you have to let her know that she is not allowed to take out her anger for someone else on you. You don't want her to get into the habit of displacing where the anger belongs."

Ulie: "How the hell do I do that with a four-year-old?"

Me: "I would like to recommend the two of you doing some play therapy. Let me give you a referral."

Small children are not my area of expertise, and I knew that Darla would benefit from play therapy. Plus, I wanted Darla to have a safe outlet for her emotions. I also wanted a therapist who specializes in working with small children to be able to document firsthand what Ulie was telling me about secondhand. Esther fought tooth and nail to prevent Darla from receiving therapy. Note: Any time a parent tries to prevent a child from receiving therapy raises huge red flags with me. Ulie and his attorney pushed the issue, and Esther very reluctantly agreed to therapy for Darla.

The divorce was ugly—and that is with a capital U. Esther fought over ever single item, every cent. She demanded full custody; when denied, she doubled her attacks with Ulie, and the play therapist was able to document the cognitive dissonance going on with Darla. Soon the unfounded accusations of incest and abuse and neglect started being made by Esther against Ulie. Esther would intentionally "forget" counseling appointments if it was her day to have Darla. Ulie was investigated, had his reputation called into question, and found innocent all the while Esther was doing what she could when she had Darla to convince her that her dad was abusing her. The divorce finally ended after almost two years of court battles. After the end of the court battle, Esther continued to attempt to abuse Ulie by proxy through Darla. Esther would bribe Darla with stuff, manipulate with guilt, and use stonewalling when she talked about her dad or said anything positive about him. The relationship with Ulie was strained as Darla struggled with pleasing her mother and spending time with her dad. Ulie nearly had a nervous breakdown as his abilities as not only a spouse but a father were called into question by his abuser; he saw the damage it was doing to Darla but could do nothing about it other than be there for her and be consistent.

As Darla grew up and found her own opinions and personality, and as Esther found a new supply and didn't want to be bothered with being a mother, the constant alienation tactic subsided. However, when Esther married again she began bribing Darla with material things to come live with her. She promised her no rules and total freedom. Her new spouse was a total flying monkey who believed every horrible story that Esther told him. As Darla became a pre-teen, the alienation tactics started up again so Darla went to live with her mother full time. Ulie was devastated as Darla told him that she "hated him for everything he had done." Darla did not have the experience or the maturity or the secure attachment to resist the lies her mother told her. Darla began to play one parent off the other.

Ulie: "I lost her. I don't know what to do now."

Me: "You did everything you could. She wants to live with her mother?"

Ulie: "Yeah. Because I enforce the rules. Esther won't. They let her get away with murder."

Me: "When you told her no, what did she do?"

Ulie: "She threatened to kill herself. She is acting just like her mother."

Me: "And you had her committed?"

Ulie: "Yes. She told the counselors she wants to live with Esther and her husband."

Me: "Are you going to do visits?"

Ulie: "Yes. Less than 50/50, and she is living with them and going to school on their side of town."

Me: "All you can do is keep speaking the truth. Actions and words have to match. Right now, she is behaving as any pre-teen would when an adult offers no rules."

Ulie: "She believes the worst of me."

Me: "I know. Right now, she does. When she is older, no longer a minor, offer her to come to counseling with you to work on your relationship."

Ulie: "What if she wants nothing to do with me when she turns 18?"

Me: "You make the offer anyway, and you keep making the offer periodically."

By the time Esther had convinced Darla to move in with her, she had turned Darla into a mini me flying monkey. Darla had learned that cutting and suicide threats got her what she wanted. Teens tend to be dramatic anyway but when a teen or a pre-teen has a parent with a personality disorder, that drama is blown out of proportion.

Ulie was heartbroken, and we had to work on who he was really, not the lies that Esther told, not the anger that Darla threw at him when it wasn't safe to be mad at her mom, but who he was and what he wanted. We worked on his childhood, his insecure attachment to his mother, his self-esteem, his mistaken beliefs that were reinforced by being in an abusive relationship. Interestingly, his first marriage was not abusive, but his wife had a terminal illness in which he was her caregiver so we also worked on codependency.

Parental alienation is heartbreaking both for the parent being dragged through the mud but also for the family and friends having to watch both the child and the parent be reabused by the abuser through their own child.

This next example of abuse by proxy is when the abuser uses the target of abuse to abuse their own family members and friends All names and identifying characteristics have been changed.

Paul, age 40, tall, blonde, works as a software engineer and Sarah, his sister, age 38, also tall and blonde, works as an administrative assistant. Both came in to see me for anxiety.

Me: "Hey guys! What did you want to work on today?"

Paul: "It's our brother Mark. He is dating this woman that none of us like."

Sarah: "He met her online, and she is just awful."

Me: "Uh, okay. Um, you said you had anxiety when I spoke to you over the phone."

Sarah: "She is abusing him, and she has started abusing us, too, through him."

Me: "Tell me more. What do you mean?"

Paul: "Mark just got out of a 20-year abusive relationship with his ex-wife Vivian. She was a tyrant. She belittled him, she accused us of all sorts of horrible things during the divorce, she tried to get us both fired from our jobs, she was just crazy."

Sarah: "So we thought that with him finally divorcing her that he was on his way to being healthy."

Paul: "But he didn't go to therapy. Instead, he got onto an online dating site and started dating. Vivian had convinced him that no one could love him but her and that no one would have him. She made him feel worthless."

Sarah: "So he meets this Thai woman online, Lilah, and she starts love bombing him immediately. Paul and I tried to tell him that she was exactly like his ex, Vivian, but he insisted that she was just like our mom."

Paul: "Yeah, it was weird. He kept saying 'Oh, you are going to love her! She is just like Mom!' Well, no! She is nothing like our mother. NOTHING!"

Sarah: "So we each went out to dinner with her and Mark, and both of our spouses didn't like her at all."

Paul: "Yeah, in fact, my wife, Marcia, turned to me and said, 'He picked another loser.'"

Sarah: "That was pretty much the sentiment of my husband, Scott. Scott said he just got a bad vibe from her. He wasn't wrong."

Paul: "So time goes on, and every time we are out together I see more and more behavior that his ex-wife had, subtly putting him down, cutting him off, making herself the center of the conversation, and always, always, talking about how much she misses her 'homeland.' She was playing up the whole foreign exotic thing like nobody's business."

Sarah: "Mark was enthralled by her, though. After each meeting, he wanted to know what we thought, and we always told him the truth. He didn't like it. She kept saying to him and to us that it was important for the family to like her because she said she knew if the family didn't like her that the relationship wouldn't work, which I thought was an odd thing to say."

Paul: "Obviously, she had a family not like her before."

Sarah: (Nodding in agreement)

Me: "So then what happened?"

Paul: "He invites her to a family dinner, and she tried way too hard for our mom and dad to like her. In fact, Mom mentioned to us she didn't like her but wasn't going to say anything because she didn't want to hurt Mark's feelings."

Me: (In my head) "Oh for fuck sake!" (Outside my head) "Did they remain silent when he was in his first abusive relationship?"

Sarah: "Yes. They didn't want to interfere and said he was an adult and knew what he was doing."

Me: (In my head) "Oh Good God! If everything was 'normal,' he wouldn't be in an abusive relationship! Drives me crazy when family members refuse to speak up!" (Outside my head) "Question? Normal childhood? Secure family environment?"

Paul: "No. Mark is the oldest from our dad's first marriage. He spent the first few years with his mom, and she was mentally ill is my understanding from Dad. Apparently, she had bipolar disorder but refused to stay on her medication. So she tried to be her own pharmacist and used alcohol and cocaine to keep herself stable, which obviously didn't work."

Sarah: "Dad was able to get custody after Mark's mom became homeless due to her drug use."

Paul: "Then Dad married our mom, and we (indicating himself and Sarah) came along."

Me: "Okay, so Mark had an insecure attachment growing up. That makes sense."

Sarah: "What do you mean?"

Me: "Well, based on what you are telling me, his early childhood was not stable, Mom was not emotionally stable, and it wasn't physically secure either."

Paul: "No. It wasn't."

Me: "That sets a person up to be in abusive relationships, especially if the parent would give sometimes and withhold at other times. That's what is called intermittent positive rewards, which is what abusers use to keep the target of abuse hooked into the relationship; it mimics the insecure relationship with the caregiver."

Sarah: "That is both of his relationships."

Paul: (Nodding in agreement)

Sarah: (Starting to tear up) "Mark isn't Mark anymore! It's like I don't know him, and he was always my supportive big brother. Now he's just a fucking asshole!"

Paul: "He was always protective of us and kind. A really good big brother—even when he was dealing with Vivian, he made time for us."

Sarah: "But the difference with Vivian is that she was gone a lot and he would see us when she was off traveling the country with her friends."

Paul: "This new woman is with him 24/7, and if he does manage to go out alone with us, she blows up his phone so that he has to be texting or instant messaging with her the whole time. I finally told him to put his damn phone down."

Sarah: "So neither Paul nor I will go out with Mark if Lilah is there. Her sense of humor is vicious. She is sarcastic. She is cruel. She is just mean."

Paul: "Suddenly, Mark's sense of humor went from gentle and funny to her kind of humor."

Sarah: "He even proudly announced that this new humor was really who he was. I said, 'No, Mark, this isn't the real you. You've never been cruel.'"

Paul: "He started pointing out everything that was wrong, instead of seeing the good in things, which was exactly what Lilah does."

Sarah: "Pretty soon, he started making us feel wrong for everything we said and did and wore and talked about. It was like it was Lilah coming out of his mouth."

Paul: "He started spouting Lilah's dislike of us. He accused us of never asking her out to dinner or having her meet our spouses."

Me: "Uh, didn't you say that you all went out for a while with your spouses to get to know her better?"

Sarah and Paul: (Nodding) "Yup! Yes!"

Sarah: "We would have time alone with him and point out the changes we saw in him and that we were concerned. And the very next time we saw him, he would put words in our mouths or say that we said things that we didn't or say we didn't say things when we did. It was crazy!"

Me: "So he was rewriting history?"

Paul: "Exactly! The worst of his was that Mom finally decided to say something so she took him out to lunch and went over all the ways that Vivian abused him, like her lying to him, trying to isolate him from family and friends, spending all of his money, putting him down, belittling anyone who pointed out her abuse."

Me: "Good for your mom! Why was that bad?"

Sarah: "Less than two weeks later, he couldn't remember having lunch with her or what was said. Like, really, truly, could not remember it. I was having lunch with him and, in a panic, he said, 'Oh my God! I forgot to have lunch with Mom!' I reminded him that he did have lunch with Mom, and he tried to blame it on stress from work. He acts confused if we point out behavior that Lilah does that Vivian did. When we do something kind for him, he acts surprised like we wouldn't normally do nice things for him."

Paul: "When his daughter had lunch with me, she called her dad to tell him what a nice lunch we had and how much she enjoyed it. Brenda, his daughter, said that he sounded surprised that she liked me."

Me: (Inside my head.) "Holy shit!" (Outside my head) "What you are describing is cognitive dissonance. In other words, his abuser is brainwashing him by gaslighting and rewriting history, making him believe the worst of you, and when information contrary to what his abuser is telling him comes in, he becomes confused and 'forgets' the information that contradicts what his abuser is telling him. That is probably why he couldn't remember lunch with your mom and why he appeared confused when Brenda talked about how much she enjoyed hanging out with you. This is also known as abuse by proxy."

Paul and Sarah: "What do you mean?"

Me: "Essentially, Mark has given up all boundaries, and Lilah is running the show. She knows you see what she is doing, and so she must eliminate you from his life because you are a threat to her being able to control him. She is lying and encouraging him to accuse you of all the things she is accusing you of doing and saying. She is encouraging him to treat you poorly on her behalf. In other words, she is getting him to abuse you for her."

Paul: "Sarah and I, and now Mom, have confronted him on Lilah's behavior and he has had to go on the defensive, and we have all caught him in massive lies. That isn't our brother! He was always upstanding and a man of his word, but now…"

Sarah: "He lies about the littlest things. He rewrites history. He believes the worst of his family or anyone, friends included, who sees Lilah for what she is. We asked him to come to counseling but he screamed at us that he doesn't need counseling, that we are immature and controlling and childish and we are the ones who need counseling. Kris, in the past, when things got wonky, he would be totally willing to work on and repair the relationship, even when he was with his first wife."

Paul: "Also, his ego is out of control. He was always grateful and humble and now he is acting like an entitled jerk. He says things like 'I am so good-looking that all the women want me' and that 'I am the reason my company is doing so well.' Like he is some sort of Adonis and the only person working at his company. It is just so out of character for him! The lying is out of character for him. The way he is treating us is out of character for him!"

Sarah: "His daughter Brenda told me that she was over at the house visiting and that Lilah was there spending the night and that Lilah started screaming at him at one in the morning and that it went until Brenda finally got her luggage and left at four in the morning. She said that Lilah was dragging up things that happened with the family in the past and tried to blame Brenda as well. That Lilah was demanding he not allow Brenda over."

Paul: "Sarah and I told him that we were not interested in continuing a relationship with him unless he was willing to come to therapy and, frankly, he needs to apologize for how he has behaved and what he has said."

Me: "That will never happen as long as his abuser is in his life."

Sarah: (Bursting into tears) "I miss my brother! I want my big brother back! I just don't understand it! How could he go from kind, loving, protective, truthful, to mean, cruel, and apparently unable to tell the truth? How? How?"

Paul: "He hates us because we refuse to accept Lilah. I will NEVER accept her! I know a fucking abuser when I see one! But Sarah is right. Why is he so invested in staying with someone like that?"

Me: "Well, there are a few things going on. One is that this relationship feels familiar and comfortable."

Paul and Sarah: "What?!"

Me: "His attachment style appears to be insecure, and he has sought out, not once, but twice, abusive relationships in which the person runs hot and cold, in which there is a great deal of drama, which he is confusing for love and passion. The other thing that is going on is that more than likely the abuser has been pumping up his ego, telling him all sorts of things like that all of her girlfriends or even female friends or coworkers of his want him and that, of course, he is the reason that the company is doing well, which a healthy person would recognize as manipulation, but he clearly is not healthy."

Paul: "But why is he so adamant that he stay in this

relationship?"

Me: "Simple. Ego."

Sarah and Paul: "Ego? How?"

Me: "His ego is running the show right now. He is totally running her story and her thoughts about the family and friends. It sounds like almost everyone has tried to tell him that this woman is not good for him. He is under the delusion that he is being noble by staying with her and also, if he leaves her, he will have to kill his ego, which she artificially pumped up. If she lied about the family, the friends, then what else did she lie about? How good he really is? How good he is sexually? What else did she lie about? That is what will be going on in his head. That is a tall order for someone to have to face, especially if they are insecure in their attachment style."

Paul: "So he would have to realize that every single thing out of her mouth was a lie?"

Me: "Yup. That is asking a lot. If he isn't ready to face the original wound, the insecure attachment, if he isn't ready to face the fact that this person lied to him on so very many different levels, if he isn't done being abused, there is not much you can do. Until he is willing to get rid of his ego and confront his fears, he is stuck. Even if he goes back to therapy, his abuser will interfere. All you can do is maintain your boundaries and do not allow her to abuse you through him. You may have to limit or cut off contact until he figures it the fuck out."

Paul and Sarah were desperate to have their brother back. Paul ended up cutting off contact with Mark when Lilah wrote him a four-page letter damning him for every good thing he had ever done for his brother and accusing him of all sorts of reprehensible stuff and then, incredibly, demanding Paul apologize to her. When confronted with the letter, Mark flew into a rage and demanded that Paul apologize to his abuser. Paul refused and asked Mark to go to counseling with him. Mark refused, called him names, and stormed out of the house. Sarah remained in touch with Mark but refused to be dragged into the abuser's bullshit. The abuser defriended her on Facebook and attempted to smear her to Mark; however, knowing that this woman was a pathological liar, Sarah copied Mark on the entire conversation—and even at that he was furious at her for not being "nice" to Lilah. Lilah continued to attempt to abuse through Mark but Sarah refused to allow Mark to treat her poorly. Sarah had some reinforcement from Mark's daughter Brenda, who also became a target of Lilah's anger when she continued her relationship and visited overnight with her own dad.

Mark had lost family members and friends to this abuser, but it wasn't enough. He was willing to give up siblings and his own child to try and appease this woman. Like I told his despondent siblings, he simply was not done being abused, and until he was, the abuse would continue.

"Rotten bosses don't get better.
Any strategy that assumes they can, is doomed."

Scott Adams

ABUSE IN THE WORKPLACE

One of the nastiest places to be abused by an abuser of any kind is in the workplace. Narcissists love power and control and, as documented by many, many studies, seem to gravitate to becoming CEOs in companies, or at least in some position of power. Borderlines who exhibit The Queen and The Witch attributes often do likewise; the lesser narcissists and borderlines tend not to gravitate to such positions. *(https://www. psychologytoday.com/blog/what-mentally-strong-people-dont-do/201610/do-narcissists-make-better-leaders)*

Abusers gravitate to leadership positions but they are not good leaders. To be a true leader you need empathy, something that abusers simply do not have. Abusers, whether they be The (malignant) Queen or The Witch borderline or whether they be a malignant narcissist—overt, covert, communal, or somatic— want to be in control, and they want to be respected. Kind of like Cartman from Comedy Central's South Park pretending to be a police officer: "Respect mah authorateeh!" And they are cartoonish in their pursuit of respect and power. However, they are also dangerous and damaging to those who have no power. And, if a livelihood is involved, you can bet they will wield the threat of unemployment like a sword. The funny thing is, most abusers, especially narcissists, have a tendency to telegraph exactly what they are going to do and in most cases underestimate the person they are targeting. They often mistake kindness for weakness and compassion for idiocy.

Also, not all abusers in the workplace are in a position of true authority. Some try to commandeer it by association as in the following case study. Again, all names and identifying characteristics have been changed.

Terri, age 24, energetic, is doing her internship for her master's degree in counseling and is seeing me for anxiety.

Me: "Hey Terri! What brings you in today?"

Terri: "I'm doing my internship, and I have this office manager who is just…God! I would say maybe has intermittent explosive disorder? Maybe?"

Me: (Smiling) "What makes you say that?"

Terri: "Because she is just batshit crazy! I was warned when I started working there that she picks on the new hires and interns. It isn't a regular counseling office; it is a medical office, and it's the owner's wife, her husband is one of the physician's there. The group I work with just rents space there."

Me: "Go on."

Terri: "So for the first few weeks everything was fine, it was like I was falling into the routine and really liked all the people I worked with. But when I met Fran, my God! My skin crawled! Like she was overly saccharine but like she was biting back bile."

Me: "Eww."

Terri: "Right? That's what I thought! So I put it aside, I mean, she was the office manager, not my supervisor, and I wouldn't really have much to do with her, so I thought."

Me: "So what happened?"

Terri: "Fran isn't there much, and no one really seems to know what exactly she does. About three weeks into being there I heard her yelling at Carla, the receptionist, at the front desk. I mean loud enough that my client was like 'What the hell is going on out there?' About 20 minutes later I ended the session and walked my client to the door. The receptionist was in the breakroom sobbing, and I mean sobbing. This woman had given her a dressing down IN FRONT of the clients!"

Me: "Oh my God! That is so freaking unprofessional!"

Terri: "I know! But the worst of it was that during the dressing down she apparently threatened to lower her pay or to fire her. Kris, this receptionist is divorced and has two very small children so she is completely dependent on this job!"

Me: "That is so not good!"

Terri: "So, apparently, after screaming at the receptionist, Fran runs back to Dr. Mitch and lays out a total bullshit version of what happened."

Me: (Not surprised) "Not surprising."

Terri: "She tells Dr. Mitch that Carla started yelling at her. There were witnesses, other staff and clients, and they all refuted her version of events. The first voice I heard raised was Fran's, not Carla's."

Me: "She was rewriting history?"

Terri: "Yes! And with each telling it got further and further from the truth."

Me: "Also not surprising, sad to say."

Terri: "Dr. Mitch did nothing! He made excuses for Fran and blamed Carla for setting her off. Nothing happened for a few weeks, and then this bitch moved from yelling at the receptionist to yelling at one of the physician's assistants. Same scenario, I hear her voice first, the PA did not yell, the incident ends, Fran runs to her husband and rewrites what happened."

Me: "That sounds like a hostile work environment."

Terri: "It totally is!"

Me: "So how is it affecting you?"

Terri: "I had a client, a social worker from New York City, a very loud, boisterous woman, who was working with the homeless population downtown, and she was dealing with some PTSD. She likes to swear a lot and loudly. I had seen her before but Fran had not been in the office. In fact, it seems Fran only comes into the office when she wants an excuse to yell at someone."

Me: "Probably. Go on."

Terri: "I'm working with this client, and she is telling me this story of one of her clients overdosing at the shelter. And she is crying and swearing up a storm and, all of a sudden, my door is being pounded on like there is some sort of emergency, and I'm like, what the fuck?"

Me: "Let me guess?"

Terri: "Yup. Fran. I turned to my client and said, 'I am so sorry for the interruption. Let me see what is going on.' I mean, honestly, the last thing I was thinking was that Fran was crazy enough to interrupt a session. I open the door and she started screaming at me that 'There will be no swearing in this office ever!' and 'I hear swearing again from you or your clients you will be fired!' What she didn't seem to understand is that I was there doing my internship and I work for the LPC group in that medical practice, not her or the doctors."

Me: "So what did you do?"

Terri: (Laughing) "I shut the door in her face, apologized to my client, and returned to the session!"

Me: "Good for you! What did Fran do?"

Terri: "Oh, she ran to Dr. Mitch and totally lied. After the session, Dr. Mitch called me into his office and started to ream me a new asshole. But I stopped him and told him Fran was lying and that I would be letting my supervisor and my school know what happened."

Me: "What did he do?"

Terri: "He started to back paddle, you know, making excuses for her, such as 'Well, you know, she comes from a bad family! She is just stressed out! The kids are driving her crazy! She hates having to work as the office manager!' Yada, yada, yada. As soon as he finished I told him none of that was an excuse to behave poorly or unprofessionally. I then went to my supervisor and told him what happened, and he told me not to worry about it, but I do. I don't think any of the staff had ever stood up for themselves before."

Me: "Sounds like you handled it okay."

Terri: "I think so, too, but about a month later she then went after the massage therapist."

Me: "And nobody at the office is challenging her?"

Terri: "No, she is going for people she thinks are powerless. Suffice to say, the massage therapist quit that day. I am just worried that this isn't the end of her bullshit. I have enough to worry about with my school and my clients without having to worry about a nut job office manager interrupting my sessions at work!"

Terri was actually doing really well, even though she was stressed out and was in a good position to deal with this abuser's insanity, as opposed to the people who actually worked there, partly because she was a therapist herself and recognized abnormal behavior when she saw it and partly because she had the backing of her supervisor and school. With her permission, I contacted her supervisor and let him know that I was working with Terri and that the office manager's behavior was absolutely unacceptable AND violated HIPPA laws by her pounding on the door, interrupting a session, and that he was placing his license at risk by allowing the behavior to continue. Also, I asked what the hell that woman was doing standing at the door listening to a session? I also encouraged Terri to confront Fran directly and not allow her to run to Dr. Mitch. Fran was CLEARLY triangulating and, as most abusers are cowards at heart and do not deal well with being called on their behavior in the moment in public, I felt this was a good tactic to end this woman's reign of terror over my client. Terri came back a month later.

Me: "Hey Terri! How are things going?"

Terri: "Well, all I can say is that Dr. Mitch is a ball-less wonder!"

Me: "What happened?"

Terri: "Well, she did it again about 20 minutes into the session, and I just slammed the door in her face. Again, she ran to Dr. Mitch, her husband, and made up a bunch of bullshit, and he started to yell at me but I cut him off and confronted Dr. Mitch. But that second time I said, 'This is not normal behavior. She either has intermittent explosive disorder going on or a personality disorder and by her interrupting my sessions she is laying this office open to a lawsuit because what the hell is she doing standing at my door listening into sessions?'"

Me: "What did he say?"

Terri: "HAH! He backed off and started making up bullshit excuses: 'Oh, she wasn't standing at your door. A little old lady patient happened to be walking by and heard the swearing and was offended…' I would have maybe bought that except he then said, 'Well, you know the walls are thin, and her desk is on the other side of your office…'"

Me: (I made the international sign language sign for bullshit) "Moooooooooooo!"

Terri: (Laughing) "Exactly! He then promised it wouldn't happen again. But…"

Me: "Oh good God! It did?"

Terri: "Yup!"

Me: "Oy Gevalt!"

Terri: "No, it turned out well. I think you would be proud of me because I took your suggestions to confront her directly in the moment. So again, I have a client who is swearing, but not badly, just expressing hurt at his relationship. So again, about 20 minutes into the session that crazy bitch pounds on my door, interrupting my session! Now, I had started warning my clients who swear that there was an issue with the office manager and that she may pound on the door and if she does, that I will model for them assertiveness and put her in her place! I would also have to end the session to deal with the situation."

Me: "Your supervisor was aware of all this, yes?"

Terri: "Yes. That was his suggestion that I end the session and deal with her."

Me: "So what happened?"

Terri: "So, Cuntawhoris Rex, which is what all of us at the office had started calling her behind her back, pounds on my door, I open it, she starts her yelling, and I yelled over her: 'YOU are out of line and OUT of control, and if you interrupt my session again, I will have your ass committed involuntarily because you are now threatening both me and my clients!' You should have seen the look on her face! Then she turned to go run to Dr. Mitch, and I told my client, 'I have to end the session. Call me to reschedule, and thank you for understanding." I followed Fran down the hall to her husband's office, and I said as loud as I could: 'You and I will talk to Dr. Mitch TOGETHER! I am not putting up with your screaming at me or anyone else anymore and then running back to your husband like a coward and lying about it!!' At which point she started crying, and as soon as we reached his office, she started trying to push her bullshit. I told her to shut up, and then I told him to shut up because he started to defend her, and I said loudly so that everyone in or out of that office could hear that I would be filing a lawsuit for a hostile work environment, that I was keeping the school informed, and that this behavior WILL stop. They both stood there mouths gaping. My supervisor heard the commotion and came in and backed me up, as did several other office workers."

Me: "Wow. So what was the outcome?"

Terri: "The office workers all started telling Dr. Mitch their stories of abuse by Fran, and he, again, backed off, making lame ass excuses for her. He took her home, and she hasn't been back to the office since."

Me: "I am so proud of you!"

Terri: "Me, too!"

Terri absolutely did the right thing. More than likely, if Fran was treating people at the office poorly, you can bet she was probably also treating her family poorly. Dr. Mitch, by Terri's account, was a very kind, gentle soul and very empathic and good with his clients; it was just that he desperately wanted his wife, Fran, to be normal but she wasn't. He was in an abusive relationship himself with her and behaved exactly like a target of abuse would—denying, excuse making, rationalizing, and not protecting office mates from the abuse. After that last incident, Terri was left alone and was able to finish out her internship. She was hired by the company she interned with, and they eventually moved offices so that Fran was never an issue again. Fran's threats were just that, threats. Dr. Mitch never acted on any of Fran's threats to demote or fire anybody, but she certainly created a hostile work environment. Terri heard later that because of her threatening to sue, Fran was kept away from the office and encouraged by both Dr. Mitch and the other doctors at the practice to see a psychiatrist and get on psych meds.

This next story of office abusers is a personal story of mine. When I lived in Los Angeles, many, many moons ago, I worked as a receptionist for a man who had been a songwriter and producer in the 1960s. Oftentimes, abusers will also have an addiction: drugs, alcohol, sex, porn, something. This man was drinking Vodka like there was no tomorrow and taking pain pills like there was no tomorrow. And eventually, he got his death wish, and there was no tomorrow for him.

When I started work there he loved to be admired and name-dropped all of the people he knew in the recording industry. Unfortunately, his last hit was sometime in the 1980s, and it was now the mid-1990s. He ran his own sales office selling computer software. He was a grandiose narcissist to the nth degree and surrounded himself with a young staff, mostly females. I wondered why he was constantly hiring new staff all the time. I soon found out why.

I became friends with one of the sales reps at the company. Tara was a pretty blonde in her 20s, single, and living the single life in LA. We will call the narcissist in question Mr. Grand. Mr. Grand started trying to court this girl. He was in his mid-50s, and as I said she was in her early 20s. This was before I started to pursue becoming a therapist, but this was one reason why I decided to become a therapist.

Mr. Grand drank too much. When he did he would start calling up staff members and demand that they listen to his latest musical composition. Usually at 2 o'clock in the morning. Yeah!

I was getting ready to go out on a Saturday morning with my then boyfriend, now husband, John. The phone rang and there was a distraught Tara on the end of the line.

Me: "Hello?"

Tara: "Oh! Thank God! You're up!"

Me: "Tara! What's up?"

Tara: "I had the most awful night last night! Mr. Grand called me at two AM drunk off his ass, and he wanted me to hear his latest song that he was just sure was going to be his next hit."

Me: "Oh. Oh dear."

Tara: "It was AWFUL! I mean, awful. The song itself was terrible and weird, and he demanded to know what I thought of it. Because I was half asleep and shocked he called me, I didn't answer fast enough for him so he started screaming at me and called me all sorts of names and threatened to fire me!"

Me: "So what did you do?"

Tara: "I just had the phone in my hand listening, and then he stopped and suddenly I hear snoring."

Me: "Wow."

Tara: "So I waited for a few minutes and just hung up. I don't know what to do."

Me: "If you want my opinion, he probably won't even remember calling you. If he was drinking that heavily and taking prescription drugs so that he fell asleep midcall, he won't even remember talking to you, let alone threatening you."

Tara: "We should do something! He is going to die!"

Me: (Sigh) "Okay, well, we have his son's information so I can contact him this week and voice our concerns for his well-being."

The morale at the office, which was run out of his luxury apartment on the beach, was at an all- time low. Mr. Grand was moody, unpredictable, and filled with rage most of the time. We would find Vodka bottles, both full and empty, stashed all around the office. The bathroom had prescription pill bottles— Vicodin, OxyContin, Benzodiazepine, Percocet, Valium, Klonopin—from at least five different doctors, all of whom I am fairly certain were unaware he was seeing the other doctors. He had two apartments in that building, one that he lived in and the one he used for his office. I could only imagine that the one that he lived in was the same way. I contacted the son, who informed me that his father could, and I quote, "Go fuck himself and burn in hell." Suffice to say, it was an estranged relationship. The son apologized to me and informed me that he had gone no contact with his father because his father had also started calling him at 3 o'clock in the morning when his office workers had hung up on him, so that the son would be forced to listen to his music and then his rants. He said his therapist told him that his dad was self-medicating either for bipolar or for a personality disorder and, since he was an active addict and abusive, to cut all communication with him until he decided to get clean. I thanked him, and when we said our goodbyes he advised me to quit and get a different job. He wasn't wrong.

A week goes by and I come into the office early to get the day going. Tara is there in tears.

Me: "Tara! What is wrong? Are you okay?"

Tara: "Mr. Grand will not stop calling me! Or hitting on me! I need this job!"

Me: (Frowning) "No, you don't. There are plenty of jobs you can get in sales in LA."

Tara: "But I am making such good money he is paying me (I can't remember what it was but it was WAAAAAAY over minimum wage at the time and about three times what I was making.) I can't leave!"

Me: (Taken aback at what she was being paid compared to the rest of the company) "Um, hon, has it ever occurred to you that he is trying to make you feel obligated to him? No one else here even comes close to making that much."

Tara: "But he told me it was because I was so good at sales!"

Me: "Tara, you are good at sales, but it is because he wants you as his romantic partner."

Tara: "He knows I have a boyfriend!"

Me: "Tara, that hasn't stopped him from hitting on you, offering you to stay rent-free here in the office, but just you, not you and your boyfriend. I don't think this is a healthy work environment."

Tara: "But the money and he brings me flowers and candy and tells me how amazing I am!"

Me: (Not knowing what love bombing was at the time) "Honey, he is old enough to be your father. No amount of money or goodies is worth crying on a Monday morning."

Tara: "You're right. I know you're right."

Tara left the job, and there was more turnover at the office. I thought for the meantime I was safe because he had never come on to me or called me at 2 o'clock in the morning. I also had a boyfriend and was not his "type." What I failed to take into account is that the only "type" that abusers have is someone who would be narcissistic supply to them—and willing to put up with their bullshit.

About a month after Tara left the company and more people had quit due to his calling them at ungodly hours, I got the phone call at 2 AM.

Me: (Groggy) "Hello?"

Mr. Grand: "Kris! Kris! Good! You're up!"

Me: "Mr. Grand, I am not up. It is 2 in the morning."

Mr. Grand: "Well, no matter. I want to play my latest song for you. I know you will appreciate it! You are the only intelligent woman there, and I value your opinion."

Me: (Thinking in my head) "Well, this is a load of crap! Value my opinion, my ass! Especially since I did try pointing out to him all of the empty Vodka bottles, which he blamed on one of the salespeople that quit!" (Outside of my head) "Mr. Grand, I will see you in six hours, can't this wait?"

Mr. Grand: "No! My genius must be appreciated!" (He proceeded to play the music. As soon as it was done, he then asked,) "Well, what do you think?"

Me: (In my head) "Sounds like the sixties mated with a rabid disco queen and died a long painful death." (Outside of my head) "It's good. Nice rhythm."

Mr. Grand: "Good!? Nice?! You fucking miserable little cunt! You know nothing about music! You stupid bitch! It's genius! What do you know about rhythm? You know nothing, you pathetic little cunt!"

Me: CLICK.

I unplugged the phone at that point and went back to sleep. I was certain, based on previous behavior, that he would not even remember the conversation. He remembered parts of it. I arrived at work at my usual time. He was there waiting for me.

Mr. Grand: "I uh, I called you last night?" (More of a question than a statement)

Me: "Yup."

Mr. Grand: "I am sorry if I said anything bad, but I took sleeping pills, and I don't always remember what I have said."

Me: (Knowing what I know now, I would have recognized that as a narcissistic apology and known that the behavior would continue.) "Okay, well, John wasn't too happy being woken up at 2 in the morning and you screaming at me."

Mr. Grand: "Yes. Of course."

I stupidly assumed that he would stop. He didn't. He continued to call me at 2 in the morning, and I finally took to just unplugging the phone when I went to bed. When I finally gave him my 2-week notice, he treated it like I was a horrible person for abandoning him, like I was committing high treason. I left not long after the Northridge earthquake and moved to Oregon with John. I was at that job for almost a year.

Why did I stay? To be honest, with my father being an alcoholic and who was himself personality disordered and an abuser, I had an insecure attachment style, low self-esteem, and I didn't trust that I deserved better. When I moved to Oregon I got in with a good therapist, Fabian Smith, and I started working on my self-esteem and attachment style. My husband, John, was and is very supportive, and I also started taking classes and reading everything I could on psychology. Once I got my self-esteem going in the right direction, John and I moved to Arizona, and I started working on my master's degree in Community Counseling. I never put up with anyone's abuse again after that, not personally, not professionally. I heard that 2 years after we moved Mr. Grand died of a massive heart attack at age 54. Broke. Alone. Hated.

"Empaths did not come into this world to be victims, we came to be warriors. Be brave. Stay strong. We need all hands on deck."

Anthon St. Maarten

13

A TALE OF TWO EMPATH TARGETS

Why is it that no two targets of abuse ever handle things alike? And what the heck is an empath anyway? The answer to the first question is: "Well, everyone is different. Different strengths and weaknesses. Different support groups. Different levels of self-esteem. Different attachment styles." The answer to the second question is: An empath is one who feels other people's emotions deeply, sometime codependently and sometimes to their own detriment. Let me illustrate by two case studies. All names and identifying characteristics have been changed.

Eric, age 25, college graduate, and working at a tech company.

Melissa, also age 25 and also a college graduate who also works at the same tech company.

Me: "Hey guys! What are we working on today?"

Eric: "Melissa and I just got into a really bad fight."

Me: "When you say really bad?"

Melissa: "Just yelling but his ex-girlfriend is playing games."

Me: "Tell me more."

Eric: "In college I dated this girl Alison, and it was kind of an on again, off again situation."

Melissa: "She treated him like crap!"

Eric: (Laughing) "Yeah. She did. She would dump me as soon as someone 'better' came along, and when they broke up, she would call me up and apologize and…"

Me: "Hoover you back into the relationship like a vacuum cleaner?"

Eric: "Exactly! It was always about her. Her wants, her needs, never about mine or us as a couple."

Me: "Okay, so what happened?"

Melissa: "Eric and I have been together for over a year. Alison was in the program with us. I saw how she was treating Eric, and I told him he didn't deserve to be treated like a consolation prize. So he and I started dating."

Eric: "As soon as Alison found out Melissa and I were dating, she started calling me and texting me and telling me how she made a mistake and wanted me back."

Me: "Holy Hoover!"

Melissa: "We had a fight because this weekend she called Eric on his cell phone. He was in the shower so I answered; she wouldn't even acknowledge me and demanded to speak to Eric. It was ten o'clock at night. I handed the phone to Eric, and he put her on speaker phone. She launched into this sob story about how scared she was because she thought there was someone prowling around the outside of her apartment and could he please come over by himself, not with me, and check to make sure no one was around."

Me: (Rolling my eyes) "Really?"

Melissa: "Really. And the worst part was that he started to tell her he would be right over!"

Eric: "She was in trouble!"

Me and Melissa: "No, she wasn't!"

Eric: "Huh?"

Melissa: "I made the international sign for cut it off. I mouthed 'Tell her to call 911.' He did. And then he got mad that I didn't want him to go over there. That is what led to our argument."

Me: "Eric, tell me a little about your family of origin."

Eric went on to tell me that his mother was very controlling, very self-centered, and very hot and cold in her interactions with the family. As long as everyone did what she wanted and behaved the way she wanted them to, then she was somewhat loving and kind. However, the second someone went against her wishes, spent time or money on themselves, the woman would launch into a poor me rant about how much she did for everyone in the family. Eric was set up for an abuser like Alison by the intermittent positive rewards his mother bestowed on him. His father was completely codependent on the mother. His father bent over backwards to make his mother happy, giving up almost everything, which made his world very small. One thing the dad refused to give up was golfing—and even that the mother tried to take away from him by claiming they didn't have the money for it. The dad was the one that worked, the mother stayed at home; it was the Dad's money and apparently because of savvy investments, they had plenty of money. But because golfing took the dad away from the narcissistic partner, she wanted him to stop golfing, even though he was retired and really enjoyed it. I was beginning to see how Eric would be susceptible to an abuser.

Me: "Eric, there are a couple of books I would really like for you to read to help you understand why you felt obligated to go 'save' Alison."

Eric: "Wait, I don't understand! Why do you say she wasn't in trouble?"

Me: "First of all, why didn't she call 911? If she were really in danger and felt threatened, she would have called 911. Secondly, she ignored that Melissa exists and asked that you come over by yourself. If you had gone over there, I can guarantee she would have tried to seduce you."

Melissa: "Hah! That is exactly what I said!"

Eric: (Nodding) "Yeah, you are right. Why didn't she call 911? And yeah, looking back, asking me to come alone does sound weird now that you say it out loud like that."

Me: "Also, you have been with Melissa for over a year, and during that year how many times has she tried to 'win' you back from her?"

Eric: "A lot. I let Melissa know every time she texts or calls me."

Melissa: "I want that bitch out of your life, Eric. She is trying to compete for your attention with me. She is disrespectful. She won't even acknowledge me when I talk to her, she has tried to suck you back into her drama and her life, and you keep letting her. I'm done. Either you block her and stop communicating with her or we are done because I deserve to be treated better than this."

Eric: (Starting to feel defensive and controlled) "But..."

Me: "Eric, Melissa is not wrong in her assertion. But before you block her, I would like you to read a few books first so you understand that this isn't just Melissa trying to control you."

Eric: (Relaxing a little) "Ok."

Me: "I want you to read The Object of My Affection Is in My Reflection: Coping With a Narcissist by Rokelle Lerner.

Eric: (Writing the suggestion down) "Ok."

Me: "The next book I want you to get and read and work is The Disease to Please by Harriet Braiker. You have the people pleaser thing going on, and I suspect it is really hard for you to say no to people. Especially someone who reminds you of your mother."

Eric: "Yeah. It is hard for me to say no."

Me: "I want you also to get The Self-Esteem Workbook by Schiraldi and start working on your self-esteem and boundaries so that it will be easier for you to say no."

Eric: "Ok."

Melissa: "I will read those books, too. We can do the self-esteem one together!"

Me: "Excellent! Same time next week?"

Melissa and Eric read the books, did the homework, recognized family of origin issues and original wounds that led to Eric being a people pleaser and having poor self-esteem and poor boundaries. Alison attempted a few more times to Hoover Eric, and he blocked her. Melissa and Eric worked on communication issues, basic assumptions, and making it safe for both to speak their minds and be heard. I taught them reflective listening and time-outs and every tool a couple needs to be successful. Eric would occasionally get sucked into a toxic friendship but, as the years passed, he was able to recognize and avoid them with success or if he got sucked in, he could get out quickly. At last contact, he and Melissa were doing great.

I love happy endings. I wish all my cases had happy endings.

They don't. Sometimes, no matter how practiced the therapist is, there is still such a thing as free will, and sometimes, no matter how much you as the family or friend love a target of abuse, sometimes they haven't learned whatever lesson it was they were supposed to learn, or they just don't feel they deserve to be happy, or the thought of confronting the original wound is too frightening and overwhelming for them to even conceive of coming out healthy on the other side of the fear. Sometimes they are just not done being abused. Sometimes the darkness wins.

Katrina, age 42, tall, vivacious, redhead, presenting issue: depressed mood/grief.

> **Me:** "Hey Katrina! What are we working on today?"

> **Katrina**: (Immediately tearing up) "I cannot stop crying. I just lost my best friend."

> **Me:** "Oh dear. My condolences. I am so sorry." (Thinking I was dealing with a death)

> **Katrina:** "Oh no! Alex isn't dead, but she might as well be."

> **Me:** (Confused) "Okay. Tell me more."

> **Katrina:** "I loved her. I loved her as surely as the sun rises in the East. I am married to a wonderful man, Garth, and I love him dearly. Alex and I just connected. She got my sense of humor, we shared the same hobbies, we just clicked. She made me laugh so hard my stomach would hurt. She was like a playmate and best friend."

> **Me:** "Platonic?"

> **Katrina:** "Oh yes! Platonic. I mean, there was definitely an attraction, but we never acted on it. Just flirting. Alex is gay." (She smiled but was still tearing up.)

Me: "Go on."

Katrina: "She was absolutely magnificent. She was kind and gentle and funny and sweet and beautiful and tall and talented and intelligent and supportive and everything I could ask for in a friend. Only (Here she paused and sobbed silently for a few moments) she couldn't see what I saw in her. I told her at one point that I absolutely adored her and worshipped the ground she walked on; she told me that I shouldn't because she didn't deserve it. That she felt sorry for her friends because she thought she was a horrible person."

Me: "Wowsers! Sounds like she had really low self-esteem!"

Katrina: "She did. She does."

Me: "So what happened?"

Katrina: "For fourteen years she treated me well, and we had a lot of fun adventures together. She was being abused by her spouse horrifically. Uma, the ex, blew up all her friendships. She lied to her about the kind of woman she was. She isolated her and tried to get rid of her connections to her family and friends, me and Garth included. She blew up her first good job. She put her down in public, making sure to sexually humiliate her and insinuate that she didn't please her in bed."

Me: "But you and Garth were able to stay friends with her?"

Katrina: "Yes. No matter how hard her ex tried to make her give us up, she stayed; Uma even tried to get me fired from my job, saying I had 'interfered' with their relationship. But HR didn't even pay attention to the letter. But then when she got involved with her next abuser, that all changed. I honestly thought she had learned, that she understood that she was worthy and that she wouldn't repeat the same mistake. I was wrong."

Me: "Oh dear. So she got away from one abuser and went into another abusive relationship?"

Katrina: "Yes. I had encouraged her to go to a therapist and work on her self-esteem. I bought her books to read to help her through the abuse of her spouse. She never did go to a therapist, but she did finally file for divorce. I introduced her to several of my girlfriends; Olivia was one, but that was a disaster because she left her to go back to her own former abuser. But when she got with Olivia, she started acting weird with me."

Me: "Weird? How so?"

Katrina: "Like, she stopped returning phone calls to me or if she did pick up she was mean. It was so not how she had been acting previously to them getting together. So I called her on the behavior and said that Olivia isn't her ex and she doesn't need to treat me like crap to prove to Olivia that she is with her and not me; neither Olivia or I are the jealous type."

Me: "Ah, so she was acting like how she had to act with her first wife who was abusive?"

Katrina: "Yes! So I got her to see that, and things went back to normal, for a while. But then on the fucking day that the divorce was finalized, fucking stupid Olivia broke up with Alex. She could not have picked a worse day to do it. Alex calls me up, sobbing that she would die alone and no one would ever love her and that divorcing the abusive ex was a mistake."

Me: "Well, we come into this world alone and we go out of this world alone. However, if we have a good relationship with ourselves, we do not fear it. Did Olivia say why she broke it off with her?"

Katrina: "I honestly don't know what the real story is. She told me she didn't like the way Alex had been treating me, even though after I talked to Alex it got better, because a few days later Olivia was back with Ruby, a chick who was an alcoholic and treated her like an option. She said Ruby was her 'soul mate.' I had heard Ruby push that she was Olivia's soul mate."

Me: "Ugh."

Katrina: "Exactly! Anyway, I tried to tell Alex she was worthy and to work on herself and that she would not always be alone. Then I introduced her to Sandy, and she moved too hard and too fast for her. Sandy got scared and backed out. Alex kept saying she was going to die alone and no one would ever love her."

Me: "Again, low self-value and esteem."

Katrina: "Yep! Alex at this point is totally brokenhearted, and instead of going to counseling like I suggested, she immediately got onto a dating website. She got online and within a week, she is dating. Within two weeks she found another abuser. This bitch, Delores, glommed onto her immediately. This woman was the antithesis of Olivia. Olivia was tall and blonde and smart and could hold her own in a debate. This troll was short and squat and not smart at all, unless you counted in how completely manipulative she was. All of the warning signs and red flags were there. Delores spent every waking minute with Alex, and if she couldn't be there in person, she was blowing up Alex's phone with texts and calls and IMs, which is exactly what her ex used to do; both of them would do it especially if Alex was spending time with family and friends. They were a couple in less than a month."

Me: (Knowing that dating websites are literally filled with predatory abusers) "Oh, not good!"

Katrina: "It gets worse. Way worse. Alex started telling me how much like me Delores is and that I will really like her because she is just like me."

Me: "Um…"

Katrina: "Right. She is NOTHING like me! Alex wanted Garth and I to meet her so we went out to dinner, and this Delores was just trying way the hell too hard. I mean, like really weird too hard. Garth turned to me after the dinner and was like, 'Holy shit, what is she thinking?' Garth said she reminded him exactly of Alex's ex. Anyway, Delores wanted to Facebook friend me before I really knew her."

Me: "Did you?"

Katrina: "No. I refused until I got to know her better. I asked her out to coffee multiple times, and each time she came up with an excuse as to why she couldn't go."

Me: "It sounds like she knew that you guys saw through her."

Katrina: "Yep! I was going to try to give her the benefit of the doubt, except that she continually refused to have coffee."

Me: "So what happened?"

Katrina: (sighing) "Alex and I were hanging out a few months later, and I tried to tell her my concern about Delores."

Me: "Let me guess. That did not end well?"

Katrina: "No. It wasn't good. She screamed at me. Like raged. She had never in all the fifteen years I had known her ever behaved like that. I pointed out how Delores was caught in several lies, how both Garth and I did not get a good vibe from her, how she appeared to be isolating Alex, and worst was the "just kidding" nastiness that she pulled with her. Delores was sarcastic and snarky, and Alex was becoming the same way, and that is simply not who she is! I also said I was concerned because she was avoiding going out alone. That last year, she treated me horribly."

Me: "What did she say or do when she was raging at you?"

Katrina: "She called me all sorts of names. I left and then she started sending me emails telling me I owed Delores an apology. I told her I owe her nothing because I didn't say it to Delores; I said it to her, and what I said was true. She then said that I never gave Delores a chance because I never friended her on Facebook and never offered to go out to coffee. I said, 'Alex, I have the texts where she keeps coming up with excuses.' It was like she was trying to gaslight me!"

Me: "Well, if it walks like a duck…"

Katrina: (Continuing) "It was obvious that she ran back to her and told her everything that I said, which is what her first wife used to demand she do. And then she wonders why Garth and I are worried."

Me: "It sounds like when she gets romantically involved, whether they are an abuser or not, she reverts to behavior she had with the first abusive wife."

Katrina: "When I pointed out I have the texts, she stopped and apologized and gave some lame ass excuse of being stressed out. I let it slide. I shouldn't have because Delores turned up the heat. Pretty soon Alex was accusing me of sexually harassing her."

Me: "What?"

Katrina: "I would always give her hugs and back rubs; we've done that since we first met fifteen years ago. She would ask me to give her back rubs! Now suddenly, it 'made her uncomfortable,' and she was the one who would ask me to rub her back or give her a hug!"

Me: "Sounds like Delores was the one who was uncomfortable."

Katrina: "For sure! Suddenly, I went from cherished best friend to public enemy number one. Alex started lying. She said, 'Well, everyone lies, you lie to your clients and coworkers.' And I'm like, 'No, Alex I most certainly do not!' and then we are out at breakfast and she looks at me and revisits the whole 'You never asked Delores to coffee' bullshit. I told her again that I had the texts and started to pull out the phone to show her. She got mad and told me to put my phone away. A few weeks later I get this crazy phone call from Delores, blaming me for everything wrong in her life, and then she hung up. And instead of backing me, Alex blamed me and said I upset Delores. Kris, I hadn't spoken to her for six months at that point!"

Me: "Projection. She needed a villain, a scapegoat and you, unfortunately, were it."

Katrina: "Things are strained between me and Alex. I don't talk about Delores, she doesn't talk about Delores. I asked her to go to therapy with me so we can strengthen the strained friendship."

Me: "Did she agree to go to therapy?"

Katrina: "Yes. We did go to therapy. I reiterate how much like her ex this Delores behaves. It pissed her off. Our counselor told her, 'It sounds like you are not done being abused yet.'"

Me: "So far it sounds like all good stuff with the therapy."

Katrina: "I thought that, too. That our friendship was getting back on track. A few weeks later, we are at dinner, me and Garth and Alex. Garth goes to use the bathroom, and Alex says, 'You know, you claim to be a Buddhist and Buddhism is all about compassion and forgiving.' I should have fucking known something was up at that point."

Me: "Okay, where was she going with that? What did you say?"

Katrina: "She wanted me to like Delores and accept her into my personal life. I said, 'Alex, I am a Buddhist, and yes, we practice compassion and forgiveness but as Pema Chodron teaches, we do not do 'Idiot Compassion' in which we allow someone to harm us over and over.' Which is what I tried to get her to understand when she was with her abusive first spouse."

Me: "What did she say?"

Katrina: "She dropped the subject. The rest of the dinner was good, but I get home to a four-page email from Delores. The first paragraph was clearly written by Alex and was an apology; however, the next word was the word 'but,' followed by four pages demanding that I apologize to her. It was obvious she had run back to Delores and told her every single thing I said in therapy, and word for word the bitch said, and I quote, 'You have accused me of being an abuser and you are interfering in our relationship.' I was like, 'Are you fucking kidding me? She is pulling a page out of Alex's first abusers playbook.' It was almost verbatim what her ex Uma had said to me. So I did not respond. I waited until I could talk to Alex and asked her to read this bullshit out loud. Garth was with me. Alex did and said, 'I don't see anything wrong with this letter.' Both Garth and I called her out, and instead of talking she started raging again. I told her that it was clear that she had run back and told Delores what was said in therapy, and then she said, 'Well, you tell Garth everything!' I said, 'No, I don't, and Garth isn't a manipulator.' She then grabbed her stuff, called me immature and childish, lied, and said she was seeing a counselor and her counselor said I was the problem. But then when I asked who her counselor was, she backpedaled and said that she owed her counselor money and couldn't see them right now, which made absolutely no sense. And when Garth tried to talk to her, she just shook her head and muttered all the way out the door how awful I was for not accepting Delores's 'apology' and said, "'I'll see you later.' As soon as the door closed, Garth said, 'No, asshole, you won't.'"

Me: "Oh, hon. It sounds like she was using word salad, trying to turn the argument back on you."

Katrina: (Sobbing again) "I've known that woman for fifteen years! FIFTEEN years! But the second that cunt came into her life, she completely changed! I don't even know her. Where did the Alex go that I met fifteen years ago? Where?"

Me: (Sighing) "I don't have her in front of me, but you say she started becoming more and more like her abuser?"

Katrina: "Yes. The lying, The gaslighting. The snarkiness. The disrespect. The denial. The hatred. I suddenly couldn't do or say anything right."

Me: "What you are describing is an ego defense. It is called 'identifying with the aggressor.'" In other words, this woman obviously reminds Alex and everyone else of her first abuser, but her ego is invested in proving that she picked a good one. Her picker is broken, and because subconsciously she knows this woman is just like her first abuser and because she is subconsciously afraid of her, she began identifying with the abuser, picking up fleas or behaviors just like Delores' in order to avoid being punished. But it sounds like she is being punished anyway."

Katrina: (Sobbing) "She doesn't deserve to be punished by anyone! I know Delores is raging at her! I know she is pushing hard for a ring. In her screamfest to me she said she was going to make it so we, me and Alex weren't friends. She did. She managed to do what her ex could not. How? I waited a couple of days, hoping Alex would come to her senses. She didn't. I sent her an email and said our friendship was over as long as she was with an abuser. I told her if Delores were out of her life and she was in therapy, Garth and I would be happy to be friends with her again. I received an email back that was clearly orchestrated by Delores. She damned me for every good thing Garth and I had ever done. Accused me of saying things I did not. Every good thing from the books, to asking her to go to therapy, was because I wanted to control her. Delores words I'm sure! No! I don't want to control Alex, but I will tell you who is controlling her! How can she not see Delores for what she is? Her family sees it. I see it! Garth sees it! Hell, even my sister who lives 2,000 miles away sees it! Delores has isolated Alex from all of her friends. She has tried to isolate her from family. She is even jealous of Alex's grown child!"

Me: "Hon, she is in denial. Because she had never done the work, because she never truly worked on her self-esteem, because she was so addicted to the drama and abuse, she couldn't, or didn't, want to see that Delores was abusing her."

Katrina: "I warned her. My husband warned her, and her response was to scream and rage at us for pointing it out. She allowed Delores to attempt to abuse me through her! The false accusations, the gaslighting, the lies, the name calling, the devaluing and discarding! I don't get it!"

Me: "That is known as abuse by proxy. Delores couldn't get to you directly because you wouldn't play, and she is a coward. Most abusers are. When you didn't give her the response she wanted to her screaming at you on the phone, she decided to get to you through Alex by acting as a slow poison in her ear. Even though she had been around you for fifteen years and went through her abuse from her ex wife, with you as a support, she couldn't see what this new abuser was doing to her. She is covert. Like a Chinese water torture she would drip lies to her."

Katrina: "Alex went from being one of the most amazingly kind people I know to being cruel and mean and vicious—and could no longer tell a truth from a lie. (Here she let that sink in and burst again into sobs.) She turned into the personality of her abuser. I asked her to go to counseling with me but she refused. Her choice of not working on herself ended our friendship."

Me: "Indeed. Her choice. All she had to do was go to counseling to work on the friendship. But remember, this was Delores's end game. She wanted Alex isolated from everybody."

Katrina: "Delores picked a fight with Alex's brother but Doug made sure to cc Mom and Dad on it so that didn't go far. The family can't stand her."

Me: "Another red flag that she is ignoring."

Katrina: "Oh, that's another thing. I am friends with Alex's brothers and sisters and parents; she tried and they don't like her so Alex made me feel wrong for being friends with them, like I did it to control her! And then she tried to tell Doug that the family really doesn't like me. Doug called his mom, and asked what they thought of me and Doug confirmed that was bullshit from Delores that the family doesn't like me."

Me: "That is Delores. She wanted to be friends so she could control. She is projecting onto you everything that is true of her."

Katrina: "She told a mutual friend that I wanted Alex all to myself and if I couldn't have her, no one could. Kris, I fucking introduced her to both Olivia and Sandy, and I am married!"

Me: "Projection. Everything she is accusing you of is something either she is doing or about to do. Hon, abusers lay out their intentions when they project. If you are listening they will tell you exactly what they intend to do."

Katrina: "I miss Alex. Not the Alex as she is now; if she had been this mean and cruel and nasty and snarky and in denial, I would never have been friends with her in the first place. I miss the woman that was my best friend for fourteen years. This last year, since she first screamed at me? It's like a different person. She hasn't been my friend for this last year. I don't know who she is, but I certainly don't like her. I miss the Alex who made me laugh and introduced me to all sorts of different ideas and food and fun. I miss that Alex who would never have been cruel to me or anyone else."

Me: "I know."

Katrina: "Why? Why can't she see what Delores is? After

everything she went through with her ex?"

Me: "Your counselor had it right. She isn't done being abused. Just like when an addict isn't done using yet. They may 'know' all the right information, but they don't want to stop using. She hasn't hit rock bottom."

Katrina: "Jesus, Kris! She has lost all of her friends! Me and Garth included! Her grown child is fed up with her! Her siblings do not like this woman! Delores is raging at her, raging at Beth Alex's 25 year old daughter; Delores has isolated Alex, she keeps her up at night screaming at her. What is her rock bottom going to be?"

Me: "I don't know, hon. Everybody's rock bottom is different. Since she is still with her abuser and she was allowing her to abuse you through her, she really left you no choice but to end the friendship in order to save yourself."

Katrina: "I feel like I've abandoned her."

Me: "You laid it out quite clearly: If she wants to continue the friendship, the abuser needs to be gone, and Alex needs to be willing to be in therapy both for herself and to repair your friendship. You did not abandon her, you saved yourself."

Katrina: "I know. It doesn't make it any less painful. There isn't a day that goes by that I don't think about her. All of the little things that make me laugh that she used to send me, or the movies that we would go to and talk about, or the political discussions, or... (She trailed off and began to cry again.) I just miss my friend. This new Alex is not my friend. I miss my friend, and I want THAT Alex back!"

Me: "For now, that Alex is gone. She is gone until she

figures out that she does not deserve to be abused, and she is gone until she is done being abused. You've let her know the road to get back to your friendship, and she will either choose to walk down it or not. All you can do is grieve, know that you did the right thing, and let her go."

Katrina: (Looking stricken) "Have I lost her forever?"

Me: "Maybe. Maybe not. It is up to her. I would strongly suggest writing her a goodbye letter, not to be sent. Do the good, the bad, the ugly, and the horrific. At the very end, let her go."

Katrina: (Sobbing) "I can't! I want my friend back!"

Me: "There is nothing that says this is permanent. If she is willing to work on herself and go to therapy, if she dumps her abuser and if she does make amends to all of the people she has hurt because of Delores, then your friend will come back."

Katrina: "What if she doesn't?"

Me: "Then you move on with your life while she decides whether or not she is done being abused. All you can do now is send her love and light and work on you being okay without her in your life. Don't wait for her. Write the letter. If she comes around, GREAT! If not, you will have started your own healing."

Katrina did not like that answer but she knew it was the only viable option for her. She ended up writing a seven-page goodbye letter to Alex in which she thanked her for the fourteen years they were best friends and all of the fun things she introduced her to, all of the laughter she brought into her life, all of the joy, all of the silliness, all of the shared hobbies. Then she moved on to that last year to when Alex began to act weird with Olivia, then she moved on to all of the gaslighting Alex did because of Delores, and finally, the nastiness that she spewed on that final day. Katrina read the letter to me, and then we took it outside and burnt it in a clay pot I keep at my office just for that purpose. Because she was struggling so hard with her grief, I referred her to Lauren Archibeque who is a neuro-linguistic programming (NLP) practitioner and life coach for a breakthrough session, which included a hypnosis session. Katrina was able to say Alex's name without bursting into tears after that and began to move on with her life without her.

"Everything will be alright in the end.
If it isn't alright, it's not the end!"

The Best Exotic Marigold Hotel

WHAT IT BOILS DOWN TO

What it boils down to is this: In working with survivors of abuse, the similarities to survivors of addiction cannot be ignored. The treatment is pretty similar. Going no contact with the abuser, which is like going cold stone sober off of drugs. In both addition and surviving abuse, the ones who survive and do not go back are the ones who do the hard work on themselves and confront the terror of their pasts. The ones who go to therapy, who read all they can on addiction, codependency, CPTSD, abuse, personality disorders, self-esteem, inner child work, attachment styles—the ones who push themselves to confront their abuser/addiction (either in their head or in the real world) and have good boundaries—are the ones who not only survive, but thrive. They are the ones who do the work and have support both financially and emotionally. They have worked on their self-esteem and go to therapy to work on the original wound and attachment style. They know on some level that they most certainly do not deserve to be isolated from family and friends, they do not deserve to be screamed at in the middle of the night and deprived of sleep, that they deserve better.

However, the ones who Ostrich (bury their heads in the sand) or Turtle, (Pull in all extremities in an effort to stay safe from the abuser.) deny, minimize, excuse, rationalize, and refuse to work on the past, let alone the present, those who refuse to read self-help books or blogs, who refuse to go to therapy, who actively seek out another relationship/addiction before getting back into relationship with themselves, are the ones who end up either back with the original abuser or they find themselves in yet another dysfunctional relationship or worse, they find a person who was just like their original abuser. In essence, they are still using their drug of choice. They are not done being abused, they are not done being addicted to the abuse and the drama.

For the family members and friends watching a loved one go through an abusive relationship or an addiction or both, it is hell. They can see the disaster looming, but the target/addict cannot and, in some cases, will tell family and friends to sod off so they can continue to use their drug of choice, their addictive behavior with the abuser, the drama, the trauma, the ego. Until they realize they do not deserve to be abused, until they treat that abusive relationship like a recovering addict would their drug of choice, they are going to continue to allow themselves to be abused, and they will continue to harm all of those who love them. The only option in some cases is to love the target of abuse from afar, much like the only option with some substance addicts is to love them from afar.

"So what can I do?" you ask. "How can I help my friend/sister/brother/family member if they are still insisting on staying in an abusive relationship?" You continue to speak the truth of what you see. They may discard you for that, just like Katrina had happened to her, or they may come around as the Hudson family's daughter finally did. You have to take the kid gloves off and stop worrying about whether or not they will discard you. They are going to do whatever it is they are going to do, and really, you have to think about how you will feel if you don't call it as you see it. I cannot tell you how many times I had family and friends lament that they didn't tell the target of abuse what they saw, how many times family and friends mourned that they didn't tell the addict how they had changed for the worst, and now it was too late. I said this in my last book and I will say it again in this book: The two sorriest words in the English language are "What if?" "What if I spoke up?" "What if I asked them to go to therapy?" "What if I had told them the truth?" "What if I hadn't been afraid of their abuser?" "What if I had pointed out what everyone else but them sees?" I don't know about you, but I think it is better to get it out there and deal with them discarding you than live with the haunting regret of "What ifs?," especially if the abuser goes on to physically harm the target.

It boils down to fear and comfort.

"What the heck you talkin' about, Willis?" I hear you say. You heard me. For the target of abuse it boils down to fear and comfort. Is your fear comfortable? Is it familiar? Are you willing to settle? Have you allowed that interior dialogue to lie to you and tell you this is all there is and this is what you deserve? In order to leave an abuser, you have to change. In order to change, you have to grow. In order to grow, you have to be outside of your comfort zone and be willing to face fears and put them to rest. You have to be willing to be alone, not in a romantic relationship WHILE you work on you. You have to face all of the fears of dying alone, being alone, etc. You have to stop letting your fear make you complacent and well, fearful.

As a family member or friend, you have to stop letting the fear of losing the target dictate how much truth you tell; you have to be consistent and always honest and sometimes brutally honest. You have to stop enabling the abuse. You have to not allow the abuser to abuse you through the target. Read all you can. Educate yourself and others on abuse/addiction. Attend support groups like Al-Anon, yes, Al-Anon. Remember: The similarities between abuse survivors and addicts are numerous. You will find good supports there and maybe even ways to do an intervention. Have good boundaries. Do not allow the abuser to use you as a flying monkey. Do not allow the abuser to abuse you in any way, shape, or form. Get your own counselor so you have emotional support as you go through the trauma of watching a loved one being abused. Even if you have to close the door on the relationship with the target because of abuse by proxy, leave the door unlocked so the target of abuse can walk back through when they are ready. Give them a clear road map to getting back into a relationship with you. Let them know that once the abuser is out of their life, they are in therapy, they have offered a sincere apology and want to work on repairing the once healthy relationship with you, you are there, and the door is unlocked.

Most importantly, participate in good self-care. Eat enough healthy food, drink enough water, exercise, and stay in touch with friends and family when you feel depressed because of what your loved one is going through. Stay strong. Be gentle with yourself.

I wish this book could have ended on a happier note. I wish I could say, "Why yes! All targets of abuse can be saved! Why yes! All of them come to their senses!" But I can't. Not all of them do. Some stay in the abuse because they think it is normal and that they deserve it. They are not done being abused. Some stay in the abuse because the abuser has put them in a financial position so they feel they cannot leave. Some stay in abuse because they are too terrified to confront that original wound and attachment style. Others wake up and get out of the cognitive dissonance and F.O.G. and leave the abuse for good. They are the ones who go to therapy and work on themselves. Keep reminding the target of abuse that it is a choice, their choice. They alone have the power to make the abuse stop, but, remember: You can lead a horse to water, but you cannot always make 'em Cha Cha.